FAMOUS
GRAVES TO VISIT
BEFORE YOU DIE

FAMOUS
GRAVES TO VISIT
BEFORE YOU DIE

SK COOPER

NEW
HOLLAND

For Rhonda,
One who shares the awe and wonder of the world as we
travel through it.

CONTENTS

Chapter 1: Politics   14

King Henry VIII (1491–1547)
Ulysses S. Grant (1822–1885)
Karl Marx (1818–1883)
Cecil Rhodes (1853–1902)
Lenin (1870–1924)
John F. Kennedy (1917–1963)
Ho Chi Minh (1890–1969)
Francisco Franco (1892–1975)
Mao Zedong (1893–1976)
Nelson Mandela (1918–2013)

Chapter 2: Arts and Literature   45

Dante Degli Alighieri (1265–1321)
Leonardo Da Vinci (1452–1519)
Raphael Sanzio da Urbino (1483–1520)
William Shakespeare (1564–1616)
Voltaire (1694–1778)
Lord Byron (1788–1824)
Ludwig van Beethoven (1770–1827)
Oscar Wilde (1854–1900)
Ernest Hemingway (1899–1961)
Sylvia Plath (1932–1963)

Chapter 3: Historic   77

Frederick III, Holy Roman Emperor (1415–1493)
Queen Elizabeth I (1533–1603)
George Washington (1732–1799)
Horatio Nelson (1758–1805)
Napoleon Bonaparte (1769–1821)
Abraham Lincoln (1809–1865)
George Armstrong Custer (1839–1876)
Louis Pasteur (1822–1895)
Lawrence of Arabia (1888–1935)
Oskar Schindler (1908–1974)

Chapter 4: Popular Music   108

Buddy Holly (1936–1959)
Brian Jones (1942–1969)
Jimi Hendrix (1942–1970)
Jim Morrison (1943–1971)
Elvis Presley (1935–1977)
Marc Bolan (1947–1977)
Ronald 'Bon' Scott (1946–1980)
Johnny Cash (1932–2003)
Michael Jackson (1958–2009)
Whitney Houston (1963–2012)

CONTENTS

Chapter 5: Infamous   **139**
James Dean (1931–1955)
Marilyn Monroe (1926–1962)
Martin Luther King Jr (1929–1968)
Sharon Tate (1943–1969)
J. Edgar Hoover (1895–1972)
Howard Hughes (1905–1976)
John Lennon (1940–1980)
John Belushi (1949–1982)
Karen Carpenter (1950–1983)
Princess Diana (1961–1997)

Chapter 6: Film and TV   **171**
Humphrey Bogart (1899–1957)
Errol Flynn (1909–1959)
Walt Disney (1901–1966)
Judy Garland (1922–1969)
Rock Hudson (1925–1985)
James Cagney (1899–1986)
Frank Sinatra (1915–1998)
John Wayne (1907–1979)
Lucille Ball (1911–1989)
Dean Martin (1917–1995)

Chapter 7: Criminal   **202**
King Richard III (1452–1485)
Ned Kelly (1854–1880)
Jesse James (1847–1882)
Wyatt Earp (1848–1929)
Clyde Barrow (1909–1934) and
Bonnie Parker (1910-1934)
John Dillinger (1903–1934)
Al Capone (1899–1947)
Lee Harvey Oswald (1939–1963)
Jack Ruby (1911–1967)

Chapter 8: Antiquity   **230**
Caesar Augustus (63BC–AD14)
Pharaoh Khufu (?–2566BC)
Tutankhamun (1342–1323BC)
Qin Shi Huang (259–210BC)
Hadrian (76–138AD)
Sedlec Ossuary (1200s)
Saint John of Nepomuk (1345–1393)
Taj Mahal (1632–1653)
Pope Innocent X1 (1611–1689)
Medici Chapels (1600s–1700s)
Auschwitz – Birkenau (1940–1945)

INTRODUCTION

What do we leave behind? For most of us, we are not able to determine what the world thought of us. What we were, what we achieved, what we have done to and for others is delivered through memory. Most of that memory is transient and embedded in history. For some, there are permanent reminders of our place in the world and history – tombs.

Some of these reminders were designed by the magnificent that inhabited the world. These are the monuments of antiquity, carved into our world by the god-kings that believed they were beyond mortal. Khufu and his pyramid that spans the Giza plateau and became a new 'horizon' to his people, the Taj and its solemn statement of the power of love, Hadrian's message of devotion to the Eternal city of Mother Rome. Personal mountains celebrating the ego of men who thought that the world would be forever as they saw it.

Most others are less imposing, statements made about us by others. The fathers of nations; Washington, Lincoln, Ho Chi Minh, Mandela are remembered in the monuments created to honour them. Elegant and sombre tombs reminding us of the sacrifices made by these men and those they defeated. Idols of screen and stage often remembered with the simplicity of a plaque featuring only their name, in stark contrast to their fame but fitting for those whose identity was defined by playing others. Warrior-kings become villains or heroes as history re-examines and judges them but despite the verdict their tombs stand as evidence of their power. Their role in our lives lasts beyond their death, like Napoleon and Nelson shaping continents and nations to their will.

Others become saints and their lives stand as exemplars for us – Saint Peter has become the literal rock of the Catholic Church, Saint John of Nepomuk's silver sarcophagus a homage to humility –graves that embody a glory beyond this world and remind us of the power of the spiritual in human existence.

For the infamous and notorious, their graves remind us of a moment in time

The Terracotta Army at the Mausoleum of the First Qin Emperor watch over and protect the emperor in his afterlife.

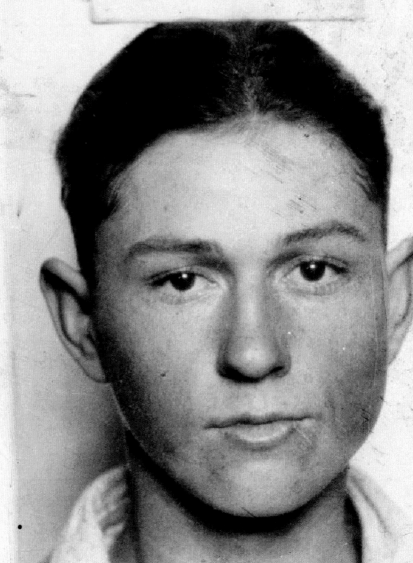

This mugshot of Clyde Barrow taken in 1926 at age 16, portends
the life of crime that would become Barrow's legacy.

– a single name is sometimes enough; 'Oswald'. Others characterise their own time and become hero or villain, it becomes us who decide; Jesse James, John Dillinger, Bonnie and Clyde, Ned Kelly – they symbolised the drive to rebel and the cost of rebellion to us all. Some reflect the beauty and happiness in our own lives; laughter and music, fantasy and fun – Disney and his mouse, Buddy and Jimi and their guitars. Some embody tragedy and waste; Marilyn. Others simply are honoured for their astonishing achievements that elevate the world and inspire humanity – Shakespeare, Dante, Michelangelo, Raphael, Leonardo and remind us of our potential, the greatness within. There are those that remind us of the twin natures of pain and beauty, hidden in us – Wilde and his tomb smothered in kisses, Morrison's garlanded bust, Plath's simple headstone.

Others are of stark elegance, symbolising the imposition of an individual's will upon the world. Rhodes' slab of granite overlooking the veldt; Marx's heavy brow staring out at us vowing to 'change the world'; Lenin unperturbed, immovable and unchanged by death in Red Square; Mao preserved in crystal perfection in Tiananmen Square.

It is the need to remember that binds us to these magnificent monuments. We honour, love, fear and admire those that have gone before us. Warriors, politicians, gods and goddesses, poets, dreamers, gangsters, bullies, musicians, artists, emperors – we are fascinated by what they have done and are driven to acknowledge them. Their tombs fix them forever in time and in memory.

Chapter One

POLITICS

KING HENRY VIII
(1491–1547)

ST GEORGE'S CHAPEL, WINDSOR CASTLE, WINDSOR, ENGLAND

Remembered as an icon of excess and self-interest, Henry VIII was the second of the Tudor dynasty and reigned from 1509 until his death in 1547. One of the most dynamic and notorious English kings, Henry's reign redefined the English monarchy by separating Kingship from Papal control, beginning the English Reformation and recasting the power of the king as divinely appointed and therefore, indomitable. He strides across history, but his fame and notoriety will be forever connected to his array of six wives. His pursuit of them, and his manipulation of the law to serve that pursuit demonstrates all that was admirable and despised of Henry.

Henry's style of kingship was quickly defined. Less than a year after assuming the throne he had his father's most unpopular ministers charged with high treason and executed. This method, Bill of Attainder, was used throughout his reign to eradicate opposition, to deflect blame and consolidate his power, and used most ruthlessly in dealing with his second wife Anne Boleyn.

An active and physically imposing man, Henry was obsessed with providing a male heir to the throne to stabilise his reign after the Wars of the Roses. This political need drove his callous manipulation of individuals and the law to achieve his goal. Infamously he redefined his first marriage to Catherine of Aragon through the manipulation of English law and had the union annulled to marry Anne Boleyn, then part of Catherine's entourage.

Anne, probably the best known of the wives, gave birth to the eventual queen, Elizabeth. Anne was married to Henry in a secret service and then later in a public wedding after Catherine had been stripped of the title. Vivacious and opinionated, Anne soon made enemies at court and her inability to produce a male heir quickly saw her being charged with adulterous treason and incest and she was executed in 1536. Henry was engaged to Jane Seymour the following day, who had been part of Anne's entourage. The same methodology Henry applied to political enemies he now used against his wives. Seymour provided the much sought after male heir, Prince Edward, but she died shortly after childbirth.

Henry wanted to consolidate his heir's position and courted Anne of Cleves for political alliances in Europe but this miserable marriage ended quickly. This resulted in another annulment, claiming the marriage had not been consummated and Henry turned on his advisor Cromwell. Henry had him attainted and beheaded for corrupt behaviour. His fifth wife, Catherine Howard soon faced the same fate, after admitting a treasonous affair. Henry married his sixth and final wife Catherin Parr in 1543. An astute woman, she reconciled Henry to his daughters and mitigated his views on religion.

Henry presented himself as the Renaissance man. Highly intelligent and well educated, his court was a literary and musical epicentre. He founded the Christ Church Cathedral School at Oxford and was reputed to have written 'Greensleeves'. Henry was much concerned with redefining the common European perception that the English were barbarians.

Enriched by the dissolution of the Catholic Monasteries, Henry used some of the funds for the betterment of the kingdom, but much was used on his war chests and his well-documented excesses, typified by banqueting that even Catherine of Aragon had commented on two decades before his death. Two hunting accidents,

separated by decades, had slowly deteriorated Henry's health, as had his tastes. His Italian-designed armour shows his 140 centimetre girth, and reports of suppurating wounds on his legs point to a range of possible illnesses and may have accounted for his violent swings of mood and rash decision-making.

Henry VIII died on January 28, 1547 at Whitehall. His last words, apparently, were 'Monks! Monks! Monks!', perhaps a reference to the compounded guilt of his destruction of Catholicism and his fear of its resurgence.

He lies with Jane Seymour beneath a marble slab. The ostentatious memorial he planned remained in pieces in England, his successors failing to honour him at such a level, as he envisioned. Such an enormous man lies simply with his wife and child, perhaps contemplating a simpler truth, a simpler life.

King Henry VIII

ULYSSES S. GRANT
(1822–1885)

GENERAL GRANT NATIONAL MEMORIAL, MANHATTAN, NEW YORK, USA

The size of the man belies his achievement and that should be his measure. General and President Ulysses S. Grant was born on April 27, 1822 in Point Pleasant, Ohio.

Grant's father was a tanner. Eschewing the disgusting processes of the family business, Grant worked on his father's farmland displaying a skill for horsemanship. He was found a placement in West Point in 1839, although disinterested in military life, he accepted the appointment to further his education. At only 5 feet tall on entry, he grew, but not substantially and graduated 21st in his class of 39. Grant showed an ability in mathematics, but was bored by military curriculum, and spent most of his time reading.

He was stationed at St. Louis where he met and married his roommate's sister, Julia Boggs Dent. He was soon involved in the Mexican War (1846–48) where he distinguished himself in battle and in his aptitude for logistics. He remarked later that it was a wicked war, and after lonely and dreary postings in California and

Vancouver he resigned from the army to settle in Missouri to farm. However, failures sent him back to his family business, disgruntled and bored.

At the outbreak of Civil War, Grant recruited and equipped troops in Galena, Illinois and he became Colonel of the 21st Illinois Volunteers, but was raised to the rank of Brigadier General almost immediately. Grant won the first Union victory at Fort Donelson in 1862 and continued with his siege of Vicksburg, with the city surrendering in 1863. Commanding all Union armies, his plan was to immobilise Confederate General Robert E. Lee's army and have Union General William T. Sherman rampage through the south. The plan worked and the war ended with another surrender at Appomattox on April 9, 1865.

Grant was immensely popular, and when he and President Andrew Johnson fell out over Johnson's manipulation of the Congress, Grant was pushed towards the Republican Party. He was elected as President in 1869 at age 46. Historians characterise Grant's administration as inexperienced, some hinting at corruption. The 'Gilded Age' was beginning and Grant's ostentatious life in the White House and his associations with corrupt Republicans, raised concerns and his second terms actions – punctuated by scandals – were bitterly regretted by Grant.

After leaving office, Grant set off on a world tour and British and German Royalty lauded him. He returned to New York after two years and an unfortunate financial speculation ruined the family and they were forced to relocate to Mount Macgregor into a simple cottage. Here he wrote his famed memoirs, while suffering the immense pain of throat cancer. He grimly finished the task and the sales went on to re-establish the family fortunes.

Ulysses S. Grant died in July 1885. A funeral cortege seven miles long accompanied his body to a temporary site in Riverside Drive. In 1897, in quiet ceremony, Grant's remains were placed inside an 8.5 tonne red granite sarcophagus inside the building. Today, Grant's Tomb remains housed in a massive mausoleum, 45 metres high.

A man judged harshly by history, Grant's worth can be summed up in his remark to Otto Von Bismark that there was no 'worse cause to fight for than the maintenance of slavery'. He was an American hero who rose to the circumstance and succeeded beyond all expectation.

Ulysses S. Grant

KARL MARX
(1818–1883)

HIGHGATE CEMETERY, LONDON,
ENGLAND

Karl Marx's famous political manuscript *The Communist Manifesto* haunted the 19th and 20th centuries in the worlds of economics and geopolitics. The imposing, squat bust of Marx's head that looks out on Highgate Cemetery symbolises the vision of one of the most influential of modern thinkers.

Forces of work and power replaced notions of position and station and electrified working classes across Europe. This fear fuelled revolution and war, and divided the continent on ideological lines for another 50 years beyond the end of World War II. Never again would the relationship between worker and employer be seen in the same way, nor would governments in their economic style and direction. In a real sense we are still 'Marxists' in the way we understand the world.

Marx was born into a wealthy Prussian family in Trier on May 5, 1818. The family was originally of Jewish origin but his father had converted to Lutheranism and taken the Prussian name of Heinrich and abandoned his Yiddish name, Herschel.

From 1830 Marx attended Trier High School where many of his teachers were liberal humanists. The political stance of the school incurred the angry wrath of the local conservative government. After a police raid the authorities instituted reforms at the school. Karl Marx graduated to the University of Bonn. his involvement in a duel meant his father insisted on a transfer to the University of Berlin, a more academic and serious institution.

In the summer of 1836 Marx became engaged to a Prussian baroness, Jenny Von Westphalen and then in October 1836, started studying law at the University of Berlin. However, Marx was drawn more to philosophy and in particular the radical leftist dialectic of the German philosopher, Hegel. This fascination lasted throughout Marx's life and would lead him to his defining works – the *Communist Manifesto* and *Das Kapital*.

Marx was becoming more radicalised and his career in the law was replaced by a need to publish and a long series appointments as editor of radical newspapers began. His agitation brought him to the attention of the German authorities, the consequence being a move to Paris in 1843, the year in which he married Jenny. It was here, in Paris, where Marx established contact with the some of the most important political dissidents of his time and his reputation as an influential writer blossomed. It was also in Paris where he met Friedrich Engels, his collaborator and lifelong friend and benefactor. Marx established his study of economics that would radically shift the understanding of capitalism; essentially that the world is shaped by actual physical activities and not by ideas, a concept that would fuel revolutions in the next half a century. Marx's activities led him to move from Paris to Brussels, being unable to return to Germany.

In this period Marx and Engels formulated the *Communist Manifesto*. The document was a call to arms and a checklist for achieving the end of capitalism and establishment of socialism in Europe. Its publication caused a storm and in the atmosphere of genuine revolutions in France and Prussia, established Marx as a danger to society. After a brief stay in Cologne, Marx was hounded out of Prussia and made for England in 1849 where he would remain for the rest of his life.

While in London Marx dedicated himself to establishing a revolutionary working class. He lived in abject poverty for several years,which took its toll on his family with only three of his children surviving into adulthood. Eventually Marx could sustain his family by writing as a European reporter for the leftist *New York Tribune* until the early 1860s. During this time Marx developed more scientific based work that became the basis for his leviathan, *Das Kapital*. It was this writing, along with some accompanying pamphlets that brought Marx some wealth and fame. Much of this writing was published continually until the 1970s.

The 1880s saw Marx's health decline and following the death of his beloved and loyal Jenny, he developed a chronic lung condition that ended his life on March 14, 1883. He died a stateless person and there were 11 mourners at his funeral. Family and friends buried him in Highgate Cemetery on March 17, 1883. Engels spoke and read two telegrams.

Marx's tombstone bears the inscription 'Workers of all lands unite!' And Engels' addition: 'The philosophers have only interpreted the world in various ways – The point is to change it'. This monument was built in 1954 by the Communist party of Britain.

There is no doubt that Engels was right, and in a sense we understand the world now as Marx wanted us to. Marx achieved that end, regardless of the consequences for world politics.

Karl Marx

CECIL RHODES
(1853–1902)

MATOBO NATIONAL PARK,
ZIMBABWE, AFRICA

Above the plains of the Matobo National Park at a place known as World View, 35 kilometres south of Bulawayo, on a granite kopke in the rolling Matopos Hills, is a granite slab covered with a brass plaque with the simple epitaph, 'Here lie the remains of Cecil John Rhodes'. Rhodes' worldview defined colonialist imperialism in Africa and he is a constant reminder, in death, of the excesses of the regimes and governments that he helped spawn. It is a gravesite distinguished by being visited by the British Royal Family because Rhodes was the man that, under the auspices of Britain, shaped colonial rule in Eastern and Southern Africa. His life and behaviour gives an insight into a type of morality and ethics that would be shunned today. It is a rare feat to have a nation named after you and rarer still to be despised by so much of that population today.

Rhodes was sent to Africa in an attempt to improve his fragile health and landed in Durban in 1870. He was tall, lanky, anaemic, shy and reserved. He was to work on his older brother's cotton farm and thereby improve his health.

The farm failed and he and his brother headed for the diamond fields of Kimberley. Over the next 17 years Rhodes succeeded in buying up the smaller mining operations in the Kimberley area. It was with the collusion of London's Diamond Syndicate, and the financial backing of the Rothschild's that his monopoly of the world's diamond supply was sealed.

Rhodes returned sporadically to England to complete his education at Oxford and inspired by a lecture by Ruskin, formed his personal mission to establish a favoured position for Anglo-Saxons throughout the world. He sought to establish British Imperialism in Eastern and Southern Africa. He turned to politics to run hand in hand with his economic and financial affairs.

His method was simplistic. He wanted to gain access for mining and development in all lands north of the Transvaal, extending to the African Great Lakes in central Africa. He achieved this through deception of tribal leadership, financial pressure and overt or covert operations with the British Colonial Office. Rhodes was directly involved in the destabilisation of the Transvaal, the outbreak of the second Matabele War and the second Boer War.

In 1889 he received a charter from the British Government to rule, police and make new treaties and concessions north of the Limpopo. In reality this allowed for the development of more enormous wealth and the establishment of an imperial zone under his control.

By the end of 1894 his company, the BSAC (British South African Company), controlled the 11,43000 square kilometres north of the Limpopo, called 'Zambasia' but known more widely from 1898 as Northern and Southern Rhodesia. He had accomplished his dream.

Rhodes' personal life was secretive and he seems only to have formed strong relationships with men, most notably Neville Pickering who died at the age of 27. Rhodes originally left his estate to Henry Currey, who later fell from his favour when he became engaged. Finally, there was Leander Starr Jameson, who nursed Rhodes in his final weeks battling heart failure.

Rhodes died on March 26, 1902 at his beach cottage in Muizenberg, Cape Colony. The government arranged for an enormous funerary train journey, stopping at every station from the Cape to Rhodesia.

His legacy is that of a man of his time; with its horrifying prejudices and morality, but he was a man who transformed the world to his own ends.

Cecil Rhodes

LENIN
(1870–1924)

RED SQUARE, KREMLIN,
MOSCOW, RUSSIA

Vladimir Ilich Ulyanov (Lenin) interpreted Marxist theory into 'realpolitik' and changed the shape and destiny of millions by leading the Bolsheviks to victory in the Russian Revolution. His ability to redefine Marxism into a working system divided a continent and fuelled the imagination of emerging leaders in Asia and Europe to unshackle themselves from their colonial pasts and challenge the world. He also set the course for inevitable confrontation with capitalism and so bound the world into a bitter and destructive divide that lasted three generations.

Lenin was born in 1870 into a wealthy middle class family that became minor aristocracy. His father's early death and the execution of his brother for anti-tsarist activities radicalised Lenin. He was qualified in the law and used his family's wealth to travel and keep ahead of the Tsarist police but he was arrested and exiled to Siberia for three years in 1893. He fled Russia and travelled in Western Europe, making extensive connections amongst the burgeoning revolutionaries in Paris, Zurich and London. Here, his anti-Tsarist writing and political theories

were refined, calling for violent widespread revolution to transform the Russian Empire totally and radically.

He returned to Russia in 1917, in a sealed train provided by the German foreign minister, to end the Russian involvement in World War I and destabilise or destroy the Tsarists. The Russian Provisional government, an interim reaction to the collapsing Tsarist government, fell in October 1917.

Lenin's radical Marxism led to unprecedented, and welcome, social and political reforms but they were countered by his establishment of the CHEKA, a brutal secret police force, and the start of a civil war that claimed the lives of millions. Eventually Soviet control was established throughout the former Russia in 1921 and recovery began with his new economic policy. The result was a mixed economy that saddled the Soviet Union with sluggish, corrupt economics for 70 years.

Lenin's health, always fragile, began to deteriorate after a failed assassination attempt. A bullet remained lodged in his throat and a series of strokes, aggravated

Lenin

by neurosyphilis, ended his life on January 21, 1924.

 Churchill commented that the Russian people's worst misfortune was Lenin's birth; the next worst was his death. Years of Stalinist horror saw the Russian people become victim to a distortion of Leninist ideals and political tools that, in effect, saw a more brutal 'Tsar' – Stalin – weigh his hand over the Russians and Eastern Europe.

Lenin's tomb is an elegant stepped pyramid structure of marble, porphyry, granite and labradorite that houses Lenin's sarcophagus, the newest version of which was designed in 1973. Mourners, worshippers, and the curious enter at one end of the mausoleum and descend into the memorial hall where Lenin's body lies in permanent state. Previously, the tomb was constructed of timber, but as technological advances in medicine allowed for more effective embalming, Lenin's body was displayed, to encourage adherence to the ideals of the revolution. Ten million people have visited Lenin's tomb since 1924.

He lies here, immutable and in a sense , immortal. The failure of his policies reminds us of the frailty of egotism.

JOHN F. KENNEDY
(1917–1963)

ARLINGTON NATIONAL CEMETERY, ARLINGTON, VIRGINIA, USA

More than any other president, JFK's life was a reflection of the zeitgeist. Feted and charming, the notion of 'Camelot' swathed the young president and his adoring wife. The manner of his death, still contentious and discussed more than a half century later, was a forerunner to the unravelling of the American Dream, exposing the fractures in a society bitterly divided and struggling to understand itself.

The elegant tomb in Arlington Cemetery where Kennedy, his wife Jacqueline and their two deceased children lay serves as a poignant reminder of the affection and tragedy of their existence. The curse that has dogged the Kennedy's since the events of Dealey Plaza in Dallas on November 22, 1963 resonates.

Kennedy was born on May 29, 1917 to businessman turned politician Joe Kennedy and socialite Rose Fitzgerald-Kennedy. As part of the influential and wealthy Kennedy family, it became apparent that his father was grooming his son's for something greater than local politics.

John was beset with ill health throughout his life. The first serious conditions emerging at the age of 17 forced him to return from his studies in London to endure long periods of recuperation at the family home and in Arizona. Despite his health problems, John attended Princeton, and then Harvard University, interspersed with travel to Europe accompanying his father (the Ambassador to Great Britain) and elder brother, Joe Jr. He graduated from Harvard in 1940.

After medical disqualification from the army for chronic back problems, Kennedy joined the US Navy and served in the Pacific, service for which he received a distinction for bravery. His successes in the US Navy set him up favourably for a political career, firstly in the Congress (with the influence of his father finding a seat for him) and later in the Senate. He was a shining light for the Democrats and with the heavy financial backing of his father, he won the closest Presidential race in history and was sworn in as the 35th President on January 20, 1961.

Kennedy's presidency stood at a crossroads for the US, characterised as 'Camelot', a new powerful beginning for Americans, and driven by a Presidency surrounded by mystique. The memory of World War II lingered but was overshadowed by the new international realities of the Cold War. Kennedy had been bullied by Khrushchev in Vienna and now had to take a stand over West Berlin and communist threats worldwide. This culminated in the Bay of Pigs disaster and the consequent Cuban blockade. Kennedy himself rated the possibility of nuclear war at 20 percent. The Kennedy administration faced growing domestic problems with an ongoing push against organised crime, as well as the racial policies in the South, and civil rights support in the North. It was from this heady mix that forces were unleashed for the most famed assassination of the 20th century. This moment, beyond all policies and political plays, defined Kennedy's Presidency.

At least three shots were heard in Dealey Plaza at 12:30pm Central Time on Friday November 22, 1963. As the famed Zapruder film shows, the final shot was fatal, blowing the President's head apart. He was pronounced dead at 1:00pm at Parkland Hospital. He was 46, the youngest President to die in office. John F. Kennedy's presidency only lasted for three short years.

A state funeral was held and a Requiem Mass at the Cathedral of St Matthew the Apostle, his body was originally placed in a small plot in Arlington National

Cemetery. Between 1964 and 1966, 16 million visited the grave. His body was moved to a permanent memorial in 1967. No president of the 20th century displayed more charisma than Kennedy, and no other presidency has been dogged by such speculation and innuendo still capturing the imagination today.

John F. Kennedy

HO CHI MINH
(1890–1969)

HO CHI MINH MAUSOLEUM,
BA DINH SQUARE, HANOI,
VIETNAM

In our post-colonial world it is hard to imagine the reverence in which liberators from colonial rule are held, and the vehemence and hatred which drove individuals to sacrifice the many for an ideal – the ideal of freedom. Wanderer, strategist, and political creature 'Uncle Ho' epitomised the struggle of a people – its ugly reality and ultimate beauty, symbolised in the enormous mausoleum that stands over the grey skies of Hanoi.

Ho Chi Minh was born on May 19, 1890 and grew up in his father's village of Lang Sen. His father was a Confucian scholar and magistrate but was demoted for cruelty. Ho was a good student and an inherent adventurer. He received a French education as well as traditional Chinese and Vietnamese studies and was involved in a student organised anti-tax demonstration in support of the peasantry in 1907 but Ho was not yet politicised.

He took a position on a French steamer as a kitchen hand and sailed to Marseille

in 1911, the beginning of a long wandering life for the next six years that saw Ho in residence in the US, England and France. It was in France in 1919 that Ho began his work with the Communist Party. By 1920, disillusioned with the dismissal of Indo-Chinese claims of self-rule after the Versailles Peace Conference, Ho began a specifically communist political education in China and the Soviet Union.

Chiang-Kai Shek's victories in China saw Ho fleeing to Thailand until he went back in 1938 to participate in military campaigns. When he returned to Vietnam he had gained vast military experience, and in 1941 he led the Viet Minh independence movement. He led many campaigns against the Vichy (Fascist) French government and the Japanese invading forces. He had garnered support from the British and the US. It was during this time that Ho's methods became more brutal. He executed close associates and friends stating 'anyone who does not follow me... will be smashed', echoing the cruelty for which his father was infamous.

The end of World War II saw an acceleration of political activity in Indo-China to redraw colonial maps. The Chinese sent a force of 200,000 to Hanoi to assert communist authority and Ho sided with French forces to oppose China, explaining, 'I would rather sniff French shit for five years, than eat Chinese shit for a thousand'. The cooperation soon broke down and Ho declared war against the French in December 1946. He formed the NVA (North Vietnamese Army), systematically destroying infrastructure and using guerrilla warfare. Assassinations reached 150,000. He secured military support from the Soviet Union, and at the Battle of Dien Bien Phu annihilated the French. By 1954 the country was divided into Communist North and Democratic South.

Ho brutally enforced 'rent reduction' and land redistribution in the North, estimates put the human losses throughout this process at 500,000. The Viet Cong launched a pro-Communist rebellion in the south and Ho built supply trails in Laos and Cambodia to support the rebellion.

By 1965 American forces had arrived in the South on their worldwide attack on Communism. What had been the Cold War in Europe became a hot one in Vietnam. The American Rolling Thunder aerial bombardment failed and the Tet offensive of 1968 drove American forces back, into eventual defeat – a defeat Ho Chi Minh

would not live to see. Ho's health had been a concern for several years, long bouts of tuberculosis and malaria during the 1930s and '40s had severely weakened him. He finally became debilitated by diabetes, which led to his eventual heart failure on September 2, 1969 at his home in Hanoi. Such was his power that no individual was left as a natural successor and his death was unannounced for two days. Six years later popular songs still affirmed his strength and the cult of personality that was erupting.

His mausoleum dominates Ba Dinh Square at 21 metres high and 42 metres wide. The structure is carved from grey granite and lined with black and red stone. Ho's embalmed body lies in the cool central hall, surrounded by visitors whose behaviour and dress is strictly controlled – an enforced sobriety for man who would brook no deviation from his view. Ho understood the beautiful-ugly process of freedom, symbolised in his tomb.

Ho Chi Minh

FRANCISCO FRANCO
(1892–1975)

Valle de los Caídos, Spain

The tomb of Francisco Franco Bahamonde is a bittersweet reminder of a time that still divides the nation. Running a totalitarian dictatorship between 1939 and 1975, Franco, was responsible for the deaths of over half a million people between 1936 and 1939 and a further 200,000 to 400,000 in concentration camps. His brutal reign was mitigated by the 'Spanish miracle' of a buoyant economy that stood as a beacon in contrast to the struggling economies of Europe between 1959 and 1974.

From a military family, Franco rose through the ranks of the navy with distinction. Viewing the destruction of the Spanish Empire and the dissolution of the monarchy from within, Franco's politics steered towards ultranationalism. Following the rise of leftist brigades in 1936 the political divide was set between the Right and Left and the bloody civil war ensued. Franco rose through the chain of command through his well-known 'barak' (good luck). He inherited command after the other senior generals were killed in air crashes. Franco quickly became his faction's only leader and was publically proclaimed as Generalissimo and

Head of State on October 1, 1936. Franco's forces, generously supplied by Hitler, held sway of the Red brigades and eventually took Madrid in March 1939. The remainder of the country fell and Franco was quick to eliminate opposition with a 'White Terror' summary execution of leftists, intelligentsia and atheists that claimed 200,000 lives between 1939 and 1943.

Franco's government was developed on a line of 'fascismo frailuno' (friar fascism), a clerical fascism that was further supported by the re-establishment of the monarchy, but without designating a monarch until 1969. All these policies were ploys to keep Franco as the sole power within the country. Franco's brutality, served upon the population by the Guardia Civil, a military police force, is widely referenced in art and literature, most notably Picasso's painting *Guernica* and

Francisco Franco

Carlos Ruiz Zafón's novel, *The Shadow of the Wind*.

In 1974, the aged Franco fell ill from various health problems and after a brief recovery his health deteriorated further battling Parkinson's disease. On October 30, 1975, he fell into a coma and was put on life support. His family decided to disconnect the life support machines on November 20, 1975.

Franco's tomb is carved into a mountain near Madrid. Franco intended the 'Valley of the Fallen' to honour those who died in the Civil War but it is often considered a monument to modern Fascism and its ideals. It was built between 1940 and 1958 by the forced labour of Republican prisoners. The Valley of the Fallen is not only the resting place of Franco. It is believed 50,000 casualties of the Civil War – both Nationalists and republicans – are buried at the tomb. Many remains were moved secretly to the mausoleum without permission. Now families, angry that their loved ones lie next to the dictator, want their remains returned to them.

The tomb itself is being considered for reassignment as a monument to the 'fallen' but who are these fallen? Franco's claim was for his tomb to be a national monument of atonement; the question is whether this was another ploy and not a recognition of the sacrifice of all political persuasions in the horror of civil war. Many seem to see Franco's tomb as a gross realisation of the ego of a tyrant.

MAO ZEDONG
(1893–1976)

TIANANMEN SQUARE, BEIJING, CHINA

In the centre of Tiananmen Square, in an exquisite crystal coffin lays the 'Great Helmsman', the body of the man carefully preserved and sheened in wax. Mao Zedong was the man who began the modernisation of the next superpower with a 'supreme' vision of the world as it should be, but in reality he was the unprincipled megalomaniac who was prepared to sacrifice 45 million for the greater good of the people.

Mao was born on December 26, 1893. The son of a wealthy farmer in Shaoshan, Hunan, Mao was brought up in the disintegrating final years of the Qing dynasty. Systems of education and behaviours were questioned by Nationalist and revolutionary leaders, and western influence was increasing in all areas of Chinese life. Mao was impressed by the military prowess of revolutionary leaders like Washington and Napoleon and spent much of his youth studying independently. Mao tried out various vocations, he was employed in a soap factory, he enrolled in the police academy, and he even attended law school. Eventually, he began

training as a teacher, but in his own view he saw himself as an intellectual. After attending Peking University for a short time as a librarian's assistant, he was placed in the intellectual epicentre as the May Fourth Movement of 1919 erupted. He helped found student organisations based on his new and fervent Marxism and went on to form the basis of the Chinese Communist Party.

Effectively, Mao had been radicalised by 1921. The Communists had thrown in their allegiance with the Nationalists to defeat the forces of conservatism. While in Shaoshan in 1925, Mao witnessed the rising political potential of the peasantry who were incensed by the shooting of Chinese nationals by foreign police forces in Shanghai. Mao devised his notion of the peasant associations that would become the backbone of his success and the basis of his greatest horrors. Mao's rising profile in the Communist party saw him hunted and harassed by government forces.

The rising power of the Nationalists and Chiang-Kai-Shek threatened Mao's peasant revolution and he was forced into a long period of political wilderness, effectively 22 years. This time was spent leading his peasant army from various bases in the vast Chinese countryside and training and employing guerrilla tactics against the Nationalist government. This strategy had four phases, the third being the most famous, known as the Long March, in 1934. The Japanese invasion of 1937, however, saw a new enemy, and Communist forces reigned against the invaders. Mao's tactics saw the Red Army swell to one million, arranged as small guerrilla units controlling the vast majority of rural China. This allowed him to attack cities after the defeat of the Japanese, and assured his strength. He proclaimed the People's Republic of China on October 1, 1949.

To consolidate China's position in the world and his own power in the party Mao launched an astonishing reform program of industrialisation and restructuring known as the Great Leap Forward. It is here that Mao's brutal dedication to policy ideals rather than humanity was revealed. His policy killed 20 million in the following four years; peasants were worked to death to meet unrealistic economic targets, and intellectuals were banished for questioning policy. The result was economic chaos. Mao's souring relations with the USSR led to a withdrawal of aid and China was floundering. Mao's answer was to launch another program,

the Cultural Revolution, to address the failures of the recent past and create an ongoing and brutal phase of revolution, based on the youth. It was, in effect, a methodology of control through committees to destroy dissent linking radical youth and the Red Army, and to sustain Mao in power. Mao's grip on China – his control of thought, economics and political direction – continued after his death and resulted in the crippled development of China as a force beyond its borders for decades.

Mao died on September 9, 1976. His mausoleum was completed on November 24, 1976 and 700,000 people completed symbolic voluntary work on its structure. Crafted from crystalline quartz taken from the sea and accompanied by stone, seeds, water and sand to symbolise the unity of the People's Republic, the coffin is non reflective, with structural precision and strength so as to defy destruction.

Much like Mao himself, his mausoleum stands defiant and undeniable, divorced from humanity.

Mao Zedong

NELSON MANDELA
(1918–2013)

MANDELA GRAVEYARD, QUNU, EASTERN CAPE, SOUTH AFRICA

Nelson Mandela, the most iconic figure of freedom and sacrifice in the latter 20th century, galvanised a set of ideals that marked the end of colonialism in Africa. Mandela united forces in popular culture and politics to establish a new order of integrity and justice. His is a legacy of ideals, as the fledgling mechanics of democracy in South Africa struggle to translate into reality, the dream of Mandela's long journey to freedom.

Born into Tembu royalty on July 18, 1918 and named Rohihlala (trouble maker), Mandela had a privileged childhood. In his own words, his upbringing was based on 'custom, ritual and taboo' that reinforced a sense of isolation from other tribes. Mandela attended the University of Fort Hare, though throughout his time there he did not develop attachments to political organisations unlike other students.

On returning to his home after leaving University, he was shocked to find his marriage was arranged. He fled to Johannesburg, and found work as a nightwatchman at Crown Mines, where he saw the results and realities of South

42

African capitalism in action. He moved to the Alexandra Township, a poverty stricken and violent place, and one that set Mandela on his chosen political path through his study of law at the University of Witwatersrand in 1943. It was here that Mandela first became aligned with the African National Congress (ANC) and became secretary of the ANC Youth League.

The 1948 general elections saw the creation of racist apartheid policy by the Afrikaner majority and the ANC responded with what became the Defiance Campaign. Mandela's politics became more radical in response to apartheid policy and he actively embraced Marxism, his speeches calling for more radical action resulted in arrests and swelling support for the ANC. He was intermittently banned from speaking and was arrested for treason in 1956, but in an embarrassing reversal for the government was later acquitted in 1961. During this time, government forces reacted violently to a Defiance Campaign demonstration (a burning of ID passes) and massacred 69 protesters at Sharpeville and declared a state of emergency.

In response, Mandela formed a new extreme group (Spear of the Nation or MK), which advocated violence and sabotage. In the press, Mandela was referred to as the 'Black Pimpernel', and this media presence, along with the radical activities of the group, continued to attract the attention of the authorities resulting in the police issuing a warrant for Mandela's arrest. When the police finally caught up with him Mandela was sentenced to five years and was further charged with sabotage and treason in the subsequent Rivonia Trial. He turned the trial into a political forum, delivering a three hour speech entitled 'I am prepared to die' and was sentenced to life imprisonment in 1964, so beginning his 27 years of incarceration.

From 1964 to 1982 Mandela served time on Robben Island, with only two contacts allowed per year and minimum contact with family (he was not allowed to attend his mother's or son's funeral). Over the next 18 years, his conditions improved gradually. Whilst incarcerated, the world began to react against the apartheid regime in South Africa. Economic sanctions hit hard and riots in Soweto in 1976 brought Mandela further attention resulting in him becoming a cause celebré.

Mandela's 70th birthday in 1988 was celebrated with an enormous concert at London's Wembley Stadium.

Mandela was transferred to Pollsmoor and then Victor Verster prison and was courted by President Botha as a less radical alternative to other black activists. Apartheid was crumbling and new President F.W de Klerk sought a peaceful solution to what was a potential bloodbath. Klerk legalised the formerly banned ANC and released Mandela on February 11, 1990. In the coming days, Mandela spoke to 100,000 people in Johannesburg's Soccer City stadium.

In 1994, Mandela led the ANC to victory in the general election. He established the Truth and Reconciliation Commission and a new democratic constitution. He did not seek a second term and retired in 1999 to become a powerful force in international relations for the fledgling democracies.

Years of incarceration had broken Mandela's health (particularly his contraction of tuberculosis) and he spent increasing time away from public scrutiny and in hospital. Persistent lung infections weakened him and he succumbed at the age of 95 on December 5, 2013. A national mourning was held for ten days.

He lies with his ancestors in their family graveyard in the Eastern Cape.

Who, among the famous, has a better claim to the term 'Father of a Nation'?

Nelson Mandela

Chapter Two

ARTS AND
LITERATURE

DANTE DEGLI ALIGHIERI
(1265–1321)

BASILICA OF SAN FRANCESCO, RAVENNA, ITALY

Considered the father of the Italian language, *Il Sommo Poeta* (the Supreme Poet) Dante was the composer of what is widely considered the greatest masterpiece of world literature, *The Divine Comedy*. Dante Alighieri's exact birth date is uncertain, but from the clues inherent in his work and his active political life, historians estimate he was born in Florence in 1265, between May 11, and June 11.

Dante's family was politically active throughout the 12th and 13th centuries; they were supporters of the Papacy in the complexities of Italian politics. Although the rival alliances between supporters of the Pope and the Holy Roman Emperor shaped the last 20 years of his life, it was an event in his early youth that transformed his life in literature. Dante was promised in marriage to Gemma di Manetto Donati, daughter of Manetto Donati, member of the powerful Donati family. However, Dante had already fallen in love with Beatrice Portinari. She was to become his muse and is the romantic interest that drives his journey into the *Inferno* and beyond, through *Purgatorio* and *Paradiso*. Despite his love for Beatrice he married Gemma and by 1300, the year the Divine Comedy is set, he had three children with his wife.

Dante first met Beatrice at age nine and fell in love with her at first sight. He met with her often after his marriage, but it appears that their love was of the 'courtly kind' with no intimacy. Regardless, his poetry investigated love, (amore) in a new way, the '*dolce stil novo*' – a style of writing that glorified love in a new sense. Beatrice died in 1290 and so, now unattainable and welded into his imagination, she became the wellspring for the *Divine Comedy*.

At this time, Dante was heavily embroiled in the political unrest characteristic of Florence and he fought in the Battle of Campaldino, defeating the opposing faction, the Ghibellines. Political control of Florence was divided on family lines and while Dante was in Rome on a diplomatic mission to Pope Boniface, his opposition backed by the Holy Roman Emperor entered Florence, destroying much of the city. His estate was seized, he was fined (and on failing to return, at the

Dante Degli Alighieri

suggestion of the Pope), he was sentenced to perpetual exile or to be burnt at the stake if he returned. (The city of Florence rescinded his exile in 2008). His attempts to return were undone by treachery and fear, and disgusted, Dante began a wandering existence between Verona, Liguria, Lucca and eventually, Ravenna. During this time he wrote vicious denouncements of his enemies in Florence, his writings condemning he and his sons to death. This spurred Dante to write with passion and vitriol about those who had betrayed him and benevolence about those who had offered protection and solace.

During his exile he began work on the *Divine Comedy* using the models of Latin literature. He set his journey in the underworld and peopled it with a wide range of contemporary and classical figures. *The Inferno* was published in 1317, the following books *Purgatorio* and *Paradiso* seem to have been published posthumously.

His life ended in Ravenna. After contracting malaria on a diplomatic mission to Venice on behalf of Prince Guido di Polenta, Dante's health deteriorated and he died in 1321 at the age of 56. He is buried in the Church of San Pier Maggiore (now San Francisco). On the tomb erected by the Venetians there appears:

'parvi Florentia mater amoris' – *'Florence, mother of little love'*

The Florentines have long sought the remains of Dante to be returned, but the custodians in Ravenna have, on occasion, hidden his bones to avoid compliance. The Florentines have built a magnificent cenotaph dedicated to Dante in the Basilica of Santa Croce. However, Dante's body lies with those that gave him shelter on the western shore of the Adriatic, not in the city that gave him his greatest love and his greatest pain.

Dante Degli Alighieri

LEONARDO DA VINCI
(1452–1519)

CHAPEL OF SAINT-HUBERT, CHATEAU D'AMBOISE, FRANCE

If any individual can symbolise an era in history, that individual is Leonardo da Vinci and The Renaissance era. No other man can be admired for the depth and breadth of thought and achievement; he is the definition of a polymath – painter, sculptor, architect, anatomist, engineer, cartographer, botanist and writer. In a time when no distinction was made between art and science, da Vinci achieved at the highest level in so many fields.

Leonardo was born illegitimate, named Leonardo di ser Piero da Vinci, to a peasant woman Catherina, and the local lord, Piero da Vinci. Little detail is known of his early years but from the age of five he lived in his father's home in Vinci where he received an elementary education in Latin and mathematics. He recorded two childhood incidents that influenced him, a kite's tail feathers brushing his face in his cradle and when older driven by curiosity, he entered a cave, despite terror of what might be inside.

At 14, the most formative event of his life was his apprenticeship to painter and sculptor, Andrea del Verrocchio. Da Vinci's association with other artistic giants had now begun. Here, his theoretical training began in drafting, chemistry, metallurgy and mechanics as well as drawing, painting, sculpting and modelling. His grasp of these was astonishing and rapid, Verrocchio was said to have laid down the brush after having Leonardo add the angelic figures to his Baptism of Christ.

In 1482 Leonardo created a superb silver lyre; Lorenzo de' Medici was astonished at the instrument he sent it as a gift to the Duke of Milan to secure a peace treaty.

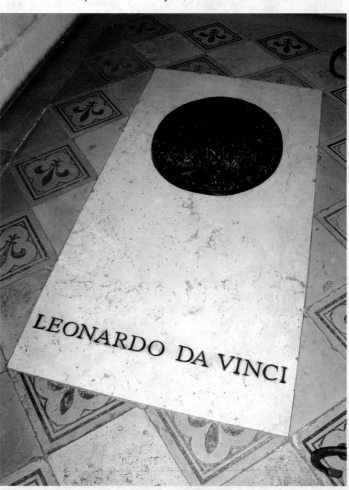

The Duke was so impressed that he retained Leonardo from 1482 to 1499 as artist and engineer and commissioned him to paint the *Virgin on the Rocks* and the *Last Supper* as well as the huge 70 tonne equestrian monument the *Gran Cavallo*. Only the *Last Supper* was finished.

The fortunes of war and politics saw Leonardo returning to Florence after

some time in Cesena, and then to Milan.

Most of his work was based on military engineering and cartography (a mystical and rare talent) however, he did create the *Mona Lisa* between 1507 and 1509 whilst in Florence. Here his work and life was bound closely to the fortunes of the Medici family (he commented that they had made him and destroyed him).

Leonardo seemed to have only formed close relationships with men – notably Luca Pacioli, the mathematician, and his pupils Salai and Francesco Melzi, who inherited his estate. At one point in time, Leonardo was charged with sodomy with a male prostitute but was acquitted, apparently under the influence of Lorenzo de' Medici.

Although not as prolific as a painter as he was in many other areas, painting has been the basis of his repute as a true genius. His techniques altered the conception of painting (particularly 'Leonardo's smoke') and his invisible brush stroking on the *Mona Lisa* is beyond compare.

Leonardo's final years were spent in France under the patronage of Francis I who became Leonardo's friend and confidant and held him as the breath left his body on May 2, 1519.

Leonardo is buried in the King's chapel in Amboise. His aloofness, genius and contradictory and diverse nature have Leonardo embroiled in controversy, simultaneously attached to the sinister and heretical Illuminati and overtly devout. One thing that cannot be challenged is his recognition as truly, a genius.

RAPHAEL
(1483–1520)

PANTHEON, ROME, ITALY

Adored by the Church and the Romans, Raphaello Sanzio da Urbino is considered by art theorists and historians to be the greatest of the three great High Renaissance artists – Michelangelo, Da Vinci and Raphael. His tomb was placed, at his request, in the Pantheon, Rome's most ancient and beautiful temple.

Born in Urbino on Good Friday in 1483, the son of the court painter to the Duke of Urbino, Raphael's precocious talent flowered in this culturally significant place. Receiving a humanist education while working with his father, he was orphaned by the deaths of his parents at the age of 11. He was under the care of his uncle, a priest, until he was placed in the workshop of the master painter, Pietro Perugino. His abilities emerged quickly, subsuming Perugino's style and developing his own. He became a 'master' in 1501, at the age of 18.

Raphael began a nomadic lifestyle, working in the northern Italian cities, spending a significant amount of time between 1504 and 1508 in Florence where Perugino had a workshop. Here, he absorbed much of Leonardo's style and, some

say, exceeded it. Many of his paintings and drawings have a similar composition but greater elegance.

After his sojourn in Florence, Raphael won commissions in Rome and came into conflict and competition with Michelangelo. It has been said Michelangelo disliked Leonardo but despised Raphael who, he claimed, had conspired against him to win commissions. In reality, Popes Julius II and Leo X set the artists against each other to create the marvels of the Vatican. The Raphael Rooms (Stanze di Raffaello) at the Vatican contain Raphael's most famous frescos and are regarded as his masterpiece. Raphael was favoured by the Popes; he was extremely prolific, running a massive workshop and working in drawings, art, architecture, and he had a diplomatic nature in contrast to the jealous Michelangelo. He was also instrumental in developing printmaking into an industry, and consequently having his work displayed across Europe.

Raphael lived a lavish lifestyle in Rome from 1508 until his death in Palazzo Caprini, and he was being groomed for greater office by his influential friends, the Medicis. He became engaged to Cardinal Medici's niece but did not marry.

Raphael's distinguished and languid art contrasted with his personal life. He is said to have had many affairs but a constant in his life was his mistress, Margarita Luti. The daughter of a baker and his model, Margarita modelled for Raphael for *The Portrait of a Young Woman* (*La Fornarina*). It was reported that he succumbed to a fever after a wild night of sex with her. Avoiding telling the Papal doctors this was the cause he was misdiagnosed and died 15 days later on Good Friday, April 6, 1520 at the age of 37. He was cognisant enough to make his funeral arrangements and enact his will, which requested burial in The Pantheon. The elite and common people of Rome attended his funeral. The inscription on his tomb, perhaps one of the most famous, written by Bembo says, 'Here lies the famous Raphael, by whom Nature feared to be conquered while he lived, and when he was dying, feared herself to die.'

He was so regarded that a process of beatification begun; reports that cracks had appeared in his Vatican work on the day of his death, and his age was changed to 33 to mirror Christ. His skull was exhibited in Accademia di San Luca, (critics were astonished to find his skull inside the tomb when it was opened in 1833).

The Church hoped to craft Raphael into the ideal of 'human and artist', and deflect criticism that he had been sacrificed for his art by its demands, as Forcellino wrote, 'compelled to paint to temper the passion that consumed him'.

Whatever the stories, whatever the reality, there are few tombs as impressive and no art more so.

Raphael

WILLIAM SHAKESPEARE
(1564–1616)

HOLY TRINITY CHURCH,
STRATFORD-UPON-AVON,
WARWICKSHIRE, ENGLAND

'Blest be man spares my bones, curst be he that moves my bones'. This rather odd and clumsy verse graces the headstone of the greatest writer in the English language, William Shakespeare. Shakespeare was the third child of eight and the eldest son of John Shakespeare and Mary Arden. Much of Shakespeare's early life is unknown but biographers agree that he was educated in Stratford and at the age of 18 he married Anne Hathaway, then 26, with whom he had three children.

Few historical traces exist until a mention in 1592 in the London theatrical scene. It was thought that Shakespeare had been a country schoolmaster and had also been in hiding after being accused of poaching Thomas Lucy's deer, about which he wrote a scathing ballad. He is also mentioned as acting in various parts. Whatever the detail, Shakespeare's plays were on the stage in London in 1592 and by 1594 were performed only by the Lord Chamberlain's Men, later known as the King's Men. Shakespeare's earliest plays, histories and comedies, were closely

based on historical publications and were seen as sensitive to the interests of the Tudor Monarchy. By the mid 1590s Shakespeare's writing became more romantic and characterisation was developing rather than staid, as was the classic mode. This trend continued with his burst of tragedies – *Hamlet, Othello, King Lear* – unparalleled in English, where concerns became metaphysical and Humanist, putting him in the forefront of the English Renaissance.

Periodically, the outbreak of plague closed theatres and allowed Shakespeare the time to create his Sonnets. Uncertain about the timing of their creation, they are recognised as a mature and intelligent observation of love and the human condition, although many of their subjects produce speculation about marital infidelity by Shakespeare.

Shakespeare's wealth had allowed him to retire from work at the age of 49 – a very unusual happening – and he returned to Stratford-upon-Avon. Within two

William Shakespeare

years he was dead. Ironically he had signed his will a month before his death, describing himself as being in 'perfect health'.

No other English writer has reshaped basic elements of the language and the art of writing. Shakespeare developed sophisticated and complex characterisation in drama, invented over a hundred new words, is the most quoted and most appropriated of writers (most English idioms can be attributed to him) and is responsible for the creation of the most elegant of speeches and expression.

As T.S. Eliot has observed, 'After Dante and Shakespeare, there is no third.' His simple tomb and his funerary monument belie his most extraordinary worth and the beauty of his creations.

VOLTAIRE
(1694–1778)

PANTHÉON, PARIS, FRANCE

Before the great movements in history, come the minds that shape the attitudes to create those events. Separation of Church and State, religious freedom, constitutional government and authority rather than absolute monarchical authority. These are all notions delivered through the acid wit and sharp tongue of Voltaire – a disaffected nobleman, a spy and a national hero.

Voltaire was born François-Marie Arouet on November 21, 1694 in Paris, the youngest of five children to François Arouet and Marie d'Aumart, a treasury official and nobleman. By the time Voltaire had left school he was determined to be a writer but his father intervened in his plans and sent him to work as a notary. Voltaire however, avoided work and spent most of his time writing essays and poetry. Despite being sent to Normandy and later to the Netherlands as a secretary to the French Ambassador (where he scandalised his family by eloping with a religious refugee, Catherine Dunoyer), Voltaire continued to write. Largely critiques of the government and religious intolerance, these activities were to result in numerous imprisonments. One verse satirising the Regent, and hinting at incest, earned

Voltaire 11 months in the Bastille, where he wrote his first play *Oedipus*.

For a variety of reasons he adopted the name 'Voltaire' in 1718, which is an anagram of his family name (he used 178 pen-names) and separated himself from his family and his past. Voltaire's behaviour, however, did not change and after insulting a French nobleman close to the Royal family he was to be imprisoned again but successfully argued for his own exile to England. The Royal family gratefully accepted, and from 1726 to 1728 he lived in Covent Garden.

In England, Voltaire's views were hardened against France's absolute monarchs. He was fascinated by Shakespeare's 'barbarism' and the relative religious freedom of the English – most particularly by Isaac Newtown and his revolutionary mathematics – as well as studies in optics and theory of gravity. These ideas he would ferment in Continental Europe on his return.

On returning to Paris he and the mathematician Condamine bought up the national lottery through a consortium, won and Voltaire, as a man of wealth, convinced the court of his reformed behaviour.

He met his great love, Émilie du Châtelet, in 1733 and their affair, of the mind and body lasted 16 years. Encouraged by Émilie, Voltaire published his 'Philosophical Letters on the English', a scathing attack on the French monarchy, and was forced to flee again, this time to Lorraine, to Émilie's château (owned by her husband, who sometimes visited his wife and her lover) in Cirey.

At the château, Voltaire and Emilie created a salon for intelligentsia, demonstrating the theories of Newton, writing his long dissertations of history and science and his poems and novels centring on religious freedom, highlighting the need for separation of Church and State as entities. This became the basis of modern political and jurisprudence systems. Here also began Voltaire's controversial correspondence with Frederick the Great, (whom he was later to spy upon at the insistence of the French government) and a period of travel to Holland, Brussels, Rheinsberg and Sanssouci; reflecting his attitude to the confining nature of the château and his inherent restlessness.

Despite his affection and commitment to Émilie he began a sexual – then emotional – relationship with his niece in Paris in 1744 and they remained together until his death. Émilie died in childbirth in 1749 and Voltaire removed himself to

Potsdam for further diplomatic relations with Frederick. Unfortunately, Voltaire's critiques and satires of German intellectuals had soured the relationship and Frederick had him arrested for a time before releasing him to the French. However, Voltaire had tried the patience of Louis XV who banned him from Paris.

Voltaire headed to Geneva, bought a large estate but his play, *The Maid of Orleans* was banned from performance (as were all plays in Geneva) and he settled in Ferney, buying yet another, larger estate and remained here until his death. Here he wrote, *Candide*, his most well-known play. He received the intelligentsia of the time – Boswell, Smith, Gibbon and Casanova – and he wrote his best-known philosophical work, *The Philosophical Dictionary*. For the first time in 20 years he returned to Paris in 1778 for a performance of his tragedy, *Irène*. He was welcomed as a national hero. The journey too much for him, he believed he was to die in February but survived until May 30. On his deathbed he famously quipped, in response to denouncing Satan, 'now is not the time to make new enemies.'

He was refused a Christian burial but he was secretly buried at the Abbey of Scellières in Champagne (his heart and brain embalmed separately). It wasn't until 1791 when he was regarded as a forerunner to the Revolution that he was enshrined in the Pantheon. One million are estimated to have attended the procession and so, after wandering and searching for justice and tolerance, Voltaire, the unimpeded wit, came home, to Paris.

Voltaire

LORD BYRON
(1788–1824)

CHURCH OF ST. MARY
MAGDALENE, HUCKNALL,
ENGLAND

If a movement in art, literature or politics can be defined through an individual then George Gordon Byron defines the triumphs of art and the excesses of the Romantics. His behaviour, so scandalous as to force him into self-imposed exile, has defied the analysis of psychologists. His literary endeavours stupendous in scale and quality, his life larger than all those that surrounded him, he is remembered by Lady Caroline Lamb's epithet, 'mad, bad and dangerous to know'.

Born in 1788, he inherited the English barony of Byron of Rochdale from his father John 'Mad Jack' Byron. His deformed foot restricted his physical development but his violent temper expressed itself in his relationships with his mother and those that surrounded him at school. He recorded his first emotional attachment to a distant cousin at the age of eight and various sources claim he was initiated into sex with a servant 'Scotch' girl at age nine and approached for sex by Lord Grey, a suitor of his mother's while still a child.

Byron seems to have been truly bisexual, forming many long term and temporary liaisons with both sexes. His years at Harrow saw strong bonds with John FitzGibbon, the 2nd Earl of Clare and others that he wrote about in his nostalgic poems about his Harrow friendships, *Childish Recollections*. These associations continued at Trinity College Cambridge, notably with John Cam Hobhouse, Francis Hodgson and John Edelston.

Byron had been writing since he was 14. His early poems received scathing reviews and his satirising of critics earned him a challenge to a duel. Byron's fame and fortune came from his poem *Childe Harold's Pilgrimage*, the first two cantos published in 1812 causing Byron to comment, 'I woke up one morning and found myself famous'. They recount his travels in Europe, skirting the Napoleonic wars and establish, in literary terms, the Byronic hero. The Byronic hero is a man disturbed by his wasted youth, who seeks some understanding and lives by wits to turn the world to his gain. Byron commented that there was no difference between protagonist and author.

Byron became the most sought after man in England. No social event was worthy without him, but his appetite for scandal and complete irreverence for convention saw him involved in a public affair with Lady Caroline Lamb and a liaison with his half-sister. His booming debt (a characteristic he shared with his father) saw him search for an heiress (another characteristic 'Mad Jack' employed). He married Annabella Milbanke but treated her miserably, and eventually he left England in 1816, never to return.

His literary fame accelerated with the publication of *Don Juan* but was outstripped by his notoriety. A range of incidents contributed to this – firstly his association with the Shelleys that spawned *Frankenstein*. Byron's seduction of married women in Venice, and his affair with the married Countess Guiccioli, led him to Ravenna where he wrote *Don Juan*, amongst other poems. There he revealed his autobiography to his publisher which was burned a month after his death, the contents of which were so scandalous as to be dangerous. His growing interest in politics drew him to Greece and the independence movement where he planned to lead a mission to attack the Turkish held fortress of Lepanto. Falling ill, he contracted sepsis after being bled, a common medical procedure

of the time, to alleviate his illness. He died in Missolonghi on April 19, 1824 at the age of 37.

Byron's body was embalmed, his heart kept by the Greeks, for whom he was a national hero. His body lay in state for two days in London and he is buried in the Church of St Mary Magdalene, Hucknall, Nottinghamshire, where a marble slab given by the King of Greece covers his grave. A duplicate slab was later placed in Westminster Abbey. It took 145 years for a memorial to Byron to be erected in Westminster; such was the daunting life and notoriety of one of England's greatest poets.

Lord Byron

LUDWIG VAN BEETHOVEN
(1770–1827)

ZENTRALFRIEDHOF, VIENNA, AUSTRIA

Revered for the astonishing feats of composing whilst deaf, Beethoven shifted emphasis and appreciation in music itself from choral to orchestral. He defined music as not simply 'pleasing sounds' but reflective of a world that it inhabits.

As with most professional musicians of the 18th century, Beethoven came from a family of professional musicians. Beethoven's family had enjoyed initial success in Bonn, Germany, before their fortunes had evaporated with the alcoholism of his father. Baptised December 17, 1770, Beethoven left school at age 11 and was the family breadwinner by 18.

Bonn had developed into a cultural capital and Beethoven was exposed to quality musical teaching and training through the Bonn court organist Christian Gottlob Neefe. He began to play viola in the Bonn opera and made such progress that he was sent for a short stint to Vienna, to study with Mozart. Mozart was impressed with Beethoven's improvisational abilities. Beethoven remained in Bonn for the next five years.

While in Bonn, Beethoven acquired a series of wealthy pupils that sustained him, as well as his virtuoso piano performances while touring Germany, this allowed him to begin composing. The German composer Joseph Haydn, whilst visiting Bonn at the time, invited Beethoven to study with him in London. This partnership failed to ignite Beethoven's imagination, and clamouring for technical and theoretical direction he set off for Vienna, the musical capital of the world in the late 18th century. It was here in Vienna where he gave his first public appearance as a pianist in 1795. He continued to compose and over the next five years gave concerts in Prague and Berlin, establishing his international reputation. His compositions were lucrative, being sought for publication and performance. However beneath this burgeoning success Beethoven had recognised a terrible reality. He was becoming deaf and wrote of his thoughts of suicide, and then of his determination to confront and defeat his affliction.

His days as a virtuoso were coming to an end and so his communication with others was restricted to conversation journals and letters, and his time was dominated by composition. This was done in sketch books on walks, some detailed, some simply a few notes, he worked unhurriedly and piecemeal and his compositions were soon becoming very lucrative. Copyright did not yet exist and Beethoven negotiated favourable deals with publishers or patrons.

His reputation in other areas was not the same. His relationships with musicians, on whom his reputation ultimately resided, became increasingly strained. Beethoven's famous cantankerousness erupted in 1808 when performances of his 5th and 6th symphonies were criticised and he threatened to leave Vienna. The Archduke Rudolf of Austria saved the situation with a generous stipend.

Beethoven's great burst of creativity developed from 1815. From then until 1827, when his deafness was most debilitating, his output slowed dramatically and he became more reclusive. Beethoven's wonderful 9th symphony took shape in 1824 with Beethoven laying on the floor with a legless piano and biting a pencil to give some acoustic awareness. His final works were created under such difficulties.

Beethoven's health began to deteriorate in 1826 and after spending the summer on his brother's estate, his return to Vienna saw him contract pneumonia, from

which he never fully recovered. He died on March 26, 1827; his cause of death was deemed to be cirrhosis of the liver. His doctor had previously performed four procedures to relieve pain in the stomach and some believe infection of the wound killed the maestro.

His last words are disputed, although his final moments were recorded and widely distributed by his sister-in-law and Anselm Hüttenbrenner. Some mention he said, 'I will hear in heaven', others say, 'Pity, pity too late' – referring to a gift of wine – and another, 'Applaud my friends, the comedy is over'.

His funeral was an enormous affair with 30,000 onlookers and many notable artists in the procession. Schubert was amongst the pallbearers for the burial in Wahring Cemetery. In 1888, Beethoven's remains were interred in Zentralfriedhof.

Beethoven's existence was unique, his creativity and virtuosity unquestioned and his genius, to overcome his affliction to rework the world of music, cannot be denied. He stands as a colossus of that special world of the musically creative.

OSCAR WILDE
(1854–1900)

PÈRE LACHAISE CEMETERY, PARIS, FRANCE

Inspirational and confrontational, Oscar Wilde was a giant of literature but, in many ways, his genius and celebrity was dwarfed by the infamy generated by his sexuality in the morally inflexible Victorian era. His grave has become iconic as a symbol of fragile genius sacrificed to the mores of the time. Until recently, the tomb famously covered in kisses, designed by Epstein and commissioned by his lover Robert Ross, was a modernist angel, depicted in relief, complete with male genitalia. The 'objects' were stolen and have been replaced by a silver prosthesis and the tomb's epitaph is a verse from Wilde's 'Ballad of Reading Gaol'

And alien tears will fill for him
Pity's long-broken urn,
For his mourners will be outcast men,
And outcasts always mourn

Wilde came from a highly privileged and intellectual Irish family, his father an honoured physician and his mother a poet. Wilde was an exceptional student and stunned his tutors at Trinity College Dublin with his mastery of Greek, French and German. It was under the tutelage of Walter Pater and John Ruskin that Wilde developed his philosophy of aestheticism. Wilde developed this ideology further when he attended Magdalene College, Oxford. His 'aesthete' featured flowing hair, scorn for sports (although he boxed) and decoration of his rooms to demonstrate his aesthetic, 'I find it harder and harder each day to live up to my blue china', he quipped.

Wilde began to write and although first attempting historical criticism, his voice was found in poetry, lectures, journalism and the stage. Now married (his childhood sweetheart had rejected him and married Bram Stoker, author of *Dracula*) he worked hard despite his aesthetic pose but his interest waned after a second child to Constance. Wilde was seduced by Robert Ross, a precocious 17 year old.

Wilde's prose writing began to bring him more fame and wealth, particularly his *Portrait of Dorian Gray*. His success on stage was unparalleled in the late 1880s, culminating in *The Importance of Being Earnest*. His work thematically dealt with what lays beneath appearance and alluded heavily to homosexuality, a crime with heavy punishments in Victorian England.

Wilde had been introduced to Alfred Douglas, an undergraduate of Oxford, in mid-1891. Douglas introduced Wilde to the underground world of gay prostitution – a world and set of circumstances that would eventually lead to his downfall. Douglas' father was the Marquis of Queensberry and questioned Wilde about his relationship with his son, challenging Wilde with a handwritten note alleging sodomy. Encouraged by his lover, Wilde took a private prosecution against the Marquis and he was arrested for libel. The Marquis hired a firm of private detectives to reveal Wilde's salacious hidden life and the trial became a nightmare for him. Wilde was arrested in 1895 but pleaded innocent to gross indecency and sodomy.

Wilde's responses under cross-examination began with witticisms and a sense of theatre but his response to a question about the 'love that dare not speak its

name' sealed his fate. Wilde described an idealised love between an older and younger man – seen as confirmation of his behaviour – Wilde was sentenced to two years hard labour, firstly in Pentonville, then in Reading gaol. With his health failing, and a fall contributing to his illness, he was released in 1897 and after short stays in Italy he returned to France where he died of cerebral meningitis in 1900. His final years were spent wandering the boulevards of Paris, sodden with absinthe, the subject of pathetic stories from Parisians and tourists alike.

Oscar Wilde

ERNEST HEMINGWAY
(1899–1961)

KETCHUM CEMETERY, BLAINE
COUNTY, IDAHO, USA

Unadorned, like his prose, a simple pink granite slab marks the remains of a writer whose influence drove the modernist movement in literature for the first half of the 20th century. The life of Ernest Hemingway became the essence of his literary imagination and his struggles with existence fuelled both controversy and admiration.

The firstborn son of Clarence and Grace Hemingway, a physician and musician respectively, Ernest was born July 21, 1899 and raised in the highly conservative suburb of Oak Park in Chicago. Hemingway's passion for the outdoors was nurtured by his father at their summer home on Lake Walloon. This was countered by his mother's insistence on cello lessons and performance in school orchestras. He excelled in English but also in sports at Oak Park and Forest High. His real passion and talent emerged in editing and writing for the school newspaper, leading him to the path of so many American novelists-journalism.

He responded to a recruitment drive by the Red Cross and became an ambulance

driver in the Italian Campaign in 1918. This experience defined his sense of mortality (a theme that haunted his writing) when he was seriously wounded. He was awarded the Italian Silver Medal of Bravery and was for the rest of life, in both a literary and literal sense, caught between the need for adventure and reality of mortal injury. This restlessness in personal relationships and physical pain he treated with alcohol. The episodes in Italy also formed the basis of much of his writing.

On return to the US to 'readjust', Hemingway found the first of his four wives, Hadley Richardson. Hemingway took a post as foreign correspondent for the *Toronto Star* and went to Paris with his bride. He soon formed close associations with the 'lost generation' of writers; Ezra Pound, Gertrude Stein, James Joyce and Henry Miller. They were all fascinated with the internal horror and complexities of existence. Here Hemingway, as well as filing articles, began his writing, reinventing the short story and began to publish to great acclaim.

After a short stint in Toronto for the birth of his first child, Hemingway returned to Europe, indulging his fascination for bullfighting and began writing *The Sun Also Rises*. He began an affair with Pauline Pfeiffer, soon to become his second wife, marrying her in 1927. While in France, Hemingway contracted anthrax and suffered a severe head injury. Determined not to live in cities, he headed to Key West in Florida, where he was to write *A Farewell to Arms*, but travelled first to Kansas City for the birth of his second child. En route to Florida he heard of the suicide of his father, commenting that he would probably go the same way. Hemingway wintered in Florida and spent his summers in Wyoming, hunting and fishing. He travelled to Europe for research, but his reckless behaviour and restlessness continued – car accidents, illnesses, amoebic dysentery, prolapsed intestine – all compounded by drinking on safaris in Kenya and Tangakiya. All found their way into his writing, dominated by the juxtaposition of contemplation and action. His craving for adventure found the Spanish Civil War irresistible and he threw himself into the Republican cause, reporting and filming the war, in the company of a young reporter, Martha Gellhorn.

Hemingway set sail for Cuba on his return to Florida and began the separation from Pauline, which led to his third marriage, to Martha Gellhorn in 1940. He relocated to Ketchum, Sun Valley, Idaho for summers and Cuba for winters, where he wrote *For Whom the Bell Tolls*, his greatest novel to date, and a stunning financial success. After the declaration of war in 1941, Hemingway had his yacht, *The Pilar*, fitted out to attack German submarines off Cuba and returned to Europe to report on the D-day landings and the Battle of the Bulge. He was subsequently charged with leading guerrilla units illegally, but received the Bronze Star for Bravery. During his time in Europe he met Mary Welsh, a reporter who became his fourth wife in 1946.

Hemingway's drinking along with the deaths of many of his literary friends and mentors culminated in his first serious bout of depression. His depression and several poor reviews led him, in a fury, to write the draft of *The Old Man and the Sea* in eight weeks in 1950. It won the Pulitzer Prize in 1952 and made Hemingway a celebrity.

Ernest Hemingway

Hemingway and Mary headed to Africa in 1954 for a disaster-ridden trip – two plane crashes had reports of Hemingway dead – his injuries were severe; burns, internal, cerebral fluid leaking from his brain pan. He survived, but his health never fully recovered. It was in this year he won the Nobel Prize in literature. He began editing material discovered in Paris that he had written in 1928, which became *A Moveable Feast*. Soon after Hemingway made a permanent move to Idaho to avoid his celebrity status in Cuba and so avoided the revolution that confiscated many of his manuscripts held there in bank vaults. His depression worsened and he was admitted for electroconvulsive therapy in 1960 and 1961.

Although widely denied at the time (to ensure a Catholic burial), in the early hours of July 2, 1961 he shot himself with his favourite shotgun, as his father had done; the restlessness at an end. The world is a different place for his writing. A man of his time and place, flawed and divide, his unique prose created a sense of fragility that Hemingway lived out in life – the bravado and a fear of death – like his beloved bullring.

He lies in Ketchum, Sun Valley, Idaho.

SYLVIA PLATH
(1932–1963)

St. Thomas' Churchyard, Heptonstall, West Yorkshire, England

Feted by feminists for her poetry and her sacrifice, her beauty hid her scarred psyche and tortured existence, Sylvia Plath was the zenith of confessional poetry. She brings to literature a work of genuine quality and a life of controversy and pain, examined from within and exposed to those outside.

Sylvia Plath was born October 27, 1932, the daughter of Aurelia and Otto Plath, in Boston, Massachusetts. Plath's father was an entomologist and professor of biology, 21 years older than her mother; his figure would shadow her early life and obsess her poetry. A gifted child, who was published by the age of eight, Plath's psyche was devastated by her father's death shortly after her eighth birthday. He had not sought treatment for diabetes and lung disease and her sense of abandonment and betrayal (read her poem 'Daddy') haunted her. Plath commented that her first nine years 'sealed themselves off like a ship in a bottle' but would ironically dominate her work in years to come. In 1950, Plath attended the prestigious Smith College and graduated *summa*

cum laude with highest honours. Her reward was an invitational editorship at *Mademoiselle* magazine in New York. The experience did not live up to her expectations, which sparked a downward spiral. A missed opportunity at meeting Dylan Thomas plunged her into depression. After slashing her legs, she received electroconvulsive therapy. Her first medically documented suicide attempt came soon after when she crawled under her mother's house and took sleeping pills; she was lying unfound for three days. Much of these episodes came to be written about in her novel, *The Bell Jar*. She was admitted to Maclean Hospital for six months and recovered obtaining a Fulbright Scholarship to Cambridge University.

At Cambridge she met her future husband, poet laureate Ted Hughes. The couple married in a whirlwind and Plath documented her love and marriage in her collection, *Colossus and Other Poems*. Plath and Hughes returned to Boston, Plath teaching at Smith but she found this was a distraction. She decided to take seminars by Robert Lowell, who persuaded her to write from experience and from a more obvious female perspective. Plath resumed psychiatric treatment and she and Hughes travelled across the US. She developed a more coherent stance to her depression but was hesitant about confessional writing.

The couple returned to Chalcot Square, Regents Park in London in late 1959 where Plath concluded her collection of poetry and her novel before moving the family to Devon. In 1961 Plath and Hughes rented their Chalcot Square flat to Assia and David Wevill. Hughes was immediately drawn to Assia and the two began an affair that was to spiral Plath into suicide. In June 1962 she attempted suicide in the form of a car accident after she had discovered the affair. The harrowing situation produced a burst of creativity with Plath, writing 26 poems, the collection *Ariel*, published posthumously. Plath and Hughes separated in September 1962.

In the winter of 1962–63, a bitterly cold one, Plath returned to London and suffering again from depression came under the care of John Horder. The doctor prescribed anti-depressants and was attending to Plath daily. At 4.30pm on February 11, 1963, Plath gassed herself. Her children were sealed safely upstairs, protected by wet towels and cloths. She was 30 years old. The feminist press vilified Hughes and her gravestone was repeatedly vandalised, the inscription Hughes had chosen scratched out and replaced with her poetry. When Hughes'

lover Assia Wevill committed suicide and gassed her 4-year-old daughter in 1969, the rage against Hughes led to death threats. The division is reflected in teaching programs throughout the world; Hughes sought answers by way of his own posthumous publication of *Birthday Letters*, a collection of poems, conversational in tone, about Plath and their marriage.

No other modern poet delved the depths and mercilessly revealed the heart and horror of a depression she described as 'talons around her heart'.

Sylvia Plath

Chapter Three

HISTORIC

FREDERICK III, HOLY ROMAN EMPEROR (1415–1493)

ST STEPHEN'S CATHEDRAL, VIENNA, AUSTRIA

Frederick III's dynasty was to extend from 1440 to 1918 and create the greatest European empire of the Middle Ages and modern times. He is buried in one of the most magnificent cathedrals in Europe and encased in one of the most important pieces of sculpture of the late Middle Ages. Adorned by the heraldry of his family and those he ruled, he is buried, with his amputated leg, in St Stephen's cathedral in Vienna.

Frederick's reign, known as 'the Peaceful', was dominated ironically by his attempts at defeating his enemies, sometimes by war, sometimes by aversion and most often through internecine intrigue. His life gives us insight into the web of relationships that dominated medieval life.

Frederick was born on September 21, 1415 in the Austrian Tyrol as hereditary Duke of Austria (Frederick V), he was elected King of the Germans in 1440 (as Frederick 1V) and Holy Roman Emperor from 1452. He quickly married the Infanta Eleanor of Portugal, using her dowry to pay debts and manipulate his power

base into supporting a war against the Swiss. He stabilised his relationship with the Papacy. Frederick controlled the world by his reluctance to change and a hesitancy to act, but was nevertheless ambitious and manipulative. To control the immensity of the Empire's territories and its competing interests he adopted a staid approach, frustrating his enemies. His personality compounded these problems, he was aloof and distant with his family and suspicious of advisers but to a large extent his problems erupted from within the Hapsburgs.

His brother Albert VI challenged his rule. Victory eluded Frederick on the battlefield, he used imprisonment of Albert's allies and his own cousins to control political tensions.

He resorted to war when necessary, (in Bohemia between 1468 and 1478) but was defeated in the Austro-Hungarian war by Mattias of Hungary, who claimed

Frederick III, Holy Roman Emperor

and occupied Vienna for five years. His victory was Pyrrhic, and he was surrounded by Viennese for his tenure. Frederick prevailed, however, outliving his opponents and confiscating their possessions. His court was a wandering affair, building castles or occupying them to subdue his enemies. Diplomatic policies centred on confiscation and marriage, rather than warfare and this delivered to him the vast area of the Empire and concessions in the West. His daughter's marriage to the Duke of Bavaria was another example of intrigue where fiefdoms were illegally taken by the Duke and the Emperor until a suitable compromise was sealed by marriage.

He had five children and for the last decade of his life he jointly ruled with his son, establishing the succession that would last for nearly half a millennium. In 1493 Frederick developed a gangrenous wound on his left foot, the foot was amputated but the gangrene remained, his leg was then amputated and he died through blood loss.

His magnificent tomb was designed and built by Nicholas van Leyden but it was not completed until two decades after his death. In the tomb is the man whose unusual vision of war and diplomacy guaranteed his bloodline for centuries to come.

QUEEN ELIZABETH I
(1533–1603)

HENRY VII LADY CHAPEL, WESTMINSTER ABBEY, LONDON, ENGLAND

Considered to be one of England's greatest monarchs, Elizabeth I, the last Tudor monarch, was born on the September 7, 1533, the daughter of Henry VIII and Anne Boleyn. Her reign of 45 years saw England survive invasion by the Spanish and wildly successful voyages of discovery and conquest. Under her auspices, the East India Company was established, the consolidation and survival of the Church of England continued amidst the flourishing of art and culture. Yet, Elizabeth's journey to the throne was fraught and dangerous. Her claim to the throne was denied when her mother was beheaded and she was declared illegitimate. Removed from the intrigues of court, she spent her formative years under the care and tutelage of a variety of powerful Protestant families. Highly intelligent (she was fluent in six languages) she was highly regarded for her personal attributes and charm. On the death of her father the throne passed to Edward VI who was aged nine but died in 1553, aged just 15. His will placed Lady Jane Grey on the throne but her reign evaporated after nine days and Mary, Elizabeth's elder half-sister, became monarch. Mary's plans to reinstitute Catholicism and marry the King of Spain disenchanted the English and popular support went to Elizabeth, but not before she was sent to the Tower for her support of the Wyatt rebellion. Her life was only spared because of a lack of hard evidence and she was moved to house arrest for a year. Mary died in 1558 and Elizabeth, at the age of 25, at last, succeeded to the throne. The Elizabethan era had begun.

Elizabeth was an autocrat, as with all monarchs of her day, but the common people loved her; she generated the perception of 'Gloriana', the personification of English resolve. This became evident in the war against the Spanish. The Armada literally floundered but the Spanish war dragged on and crippled the English economy in many respects. Elizabeth consolidated support, however, and her imposing appearance and lavish gowns exemplified the 'sacrifice' of her life as the 'Virgin Queen.' Plots against her life confirmed this notion of noble sacrifice,

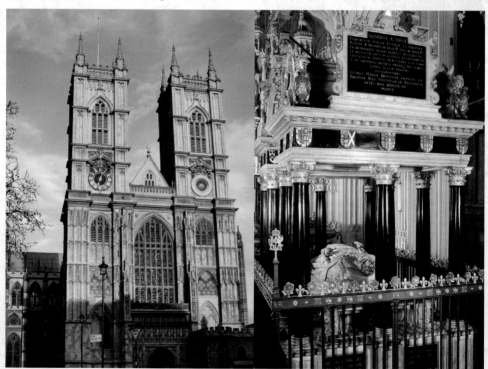

Queen Elizabeth I

particularly that of Mary Queen of Scots who had fled to England and became a focal point for Catholic rebellion led by the Spanish king. Mary was tried, found guilty and executed.

Elizabeth's 'virgin' existence was in fact an informed and shrewd political stance. Being married to either an English lord or a European prince would have made a difficult existence diabolically complex. In essence she was married to the nation and expressed this in the Golden Speech to the Commons in 1601. 'There is no jewel...which I set before this jewel; your love.'

Her death came at Richmond Palace on March 24, 1603. Her body was transported by barge to Whitehall and then to Westminster Abbey. Her body was encased in lead within a wooden coffin and was placed to the north aisle of the Abbey in 1606 and laid on top of her half-sister Mary. James I constructed the large white marble monument, reflecting the Queen in her old age. The crown and sceptre she holds are replicas, the originals having been stolen.

Elizabeth I was 'wonderfully ravished' by the populace on her accession and lays before them, ironically, a virgin in death.

GEORGE WASHINGTON
(1732–1799)

MOUNT VERNON,
VIRGINIA, USA

Few historical figures have the right, the authority and the moral stature to claim the fatherhood of a nation, yet this is the case with George Washington. Commander in Chief of forces that liberated a nation, the first leader to fight against colonisation with success, framer of political and legal institutions and the first President of the United States. Washington was more than a man of his times. He asserted the will of a people and converted that into a new reality.

Washington was born of English settlers on February 22, 1732 in Westmoreland, Virginia, British America and spent much of his boyhood at Ferry Farm near Fredericksburg. His father died when George was 11 and he came under the care of William Fairfax, a powerful figure in Virginia, and was eventually appointed Surveyor of Culpepper County, a position that gave him financial security. He was closely influenced by his uncle Lawrence, whose position of Major in the Virginia militia he inherited after his death. This led directly to his first military

engagement against the French forces occupying the Ohio valley. He was captured by the French but released to return to Virginia and by 1755 he was involved in support of British forces in their losses to the French. Washington gained notoriety for battlefield bravery and audacity and so he was given charge of the first full time American military unit, a valuable lesson he would use in the coming American Revolution. Exposure to and learning from British tactics taught him their strengths and weaknesses and consolidated his leadership qualities.

In 1759, Washington married and consolidated his vast landholdings and developed political allies from his home in Mount Vernon. It was at this time he began to agitate against the growing taxation of the American colonies formulated in the Fairfax Resolves. Washington was elected to the First Continental Congress that pushed the Colonies into a war stance with the British, erupting in the battles of Lexington and Concord near Boston. Appearing in military uniform at the 2nd Congress he was appointed Commander in Chief and led the Colonial armies. He shaped the militias into a standing army (of great importance), fought and lost but won fundamental battles at Boston, Saratoga and Yorktown (with French support). Politically, he was the figurehead for revolution. When the British surrendered, all looked to Washington to establish the fledgling republic.

It was widely thought that Washington would establish some version of monarchy but he stunned the wider world by demobilising his army and establishing the Constitution of the Unites States through a Constitutional convention. The Presidency was designed with Washington in mind and the Electoral College elected Washington on April 30, 1789, carefully avoiding the trappings of European office he was addressed as Mr President. An able administrator and astute politician, Washington isolated the Unites States from European war by neutrality agreements, allowing the States to develop and maintain economic strength. His farewell statement, published as a letter to the citizens, began a mainstay of American politics – isolationism.

Retiring in 1797, he returned to business interests at Mount Vernon. Barely two years later Washington fell ill while attending to orchards in the February snow. His doctors, on his insistence, used bloodletting and an enormous quantity of blood loss required an emergency tracheotomy to treat Washington's severely

infected throat – but this was rejected. Although still disputed as to its cause, the first President of the Republic of the United States died on December 14, 1799 aged 67.

Washington's body was interred at Mount Vernon and reinterred in a new crypt in 1837 with his ancestors and wife, the inner vault's key was thrown into the Potomac.

George Washington

HORATIO NELSON
(1758–1805)

St Paul's Cathedral, London, England

From genteel poverty to the hero of the nation, from raw recruit to bold Admiral, Horatio Nelson's 47 years set the imagination of youth wild and defined the bold and heroic defender of a nation.

Born into a Norfolk family in Burnham, Thorpe on the September 29, 1758 to a quiet English rector, Nelson was the sixth of 11 children. He was named after his godfather, Horatio Walpole, he was the great, grandnephew of Robert Walpole, Prime Minister of England. Educated at King Edward VI's Grammar School in Norwich he was set for naval service, his uncle being Maurice Suckling, soon to become controller of the British Navy.

His early naval life was routine until he was sent to the West Indies. A dangerous enough place (the British navy was at war with the American colonies), his first action was in transit in the Indian Ocean. Struck down with malaria while on a scientific expedition he was sent home to recover; it was reported that after the bout of depression that accompanied the condition he felt a surge of optimism

that drove him for the remainder of his life.

Nelson was promoted to captain at the age of 20, and in command of a frigate took to harrying the American colonies and their possessions. In 1784 he set off again to the West Indies and his staunch enforcement of the Navigation Act saw him lose favour with merchants flouting the boycott of the colonies. On his return he failed to find another command for five years, and spent this time with his new wife and adopted child.

The death of Louis XVI dramatically changed Nelson's life. He was recalled to active duty within days and given command of the 64-gun *HMS Agamemnon* and sent to the Mediterranean to defend British possessions. Here Nelson ran to Naples to collect reinforcements (he also met the love of his life, Emma Hamilton), then to Corsica where he lost the sight if his right eye in the attack on Bastia and Calvi (1794). Eventually, he went to Gibraltar to consolidate British forces.

It was on February 4, 1797 that Nelson fought the battle of St Vincent. Finding himself in mist between two Spanish squadrons, he fought and destroyed the Spanish with accurate British gunnery and boarded two Spanish men-o-war. He received a knighthood as reward and in a subsequent assault on Tenerife lost his right arm. Recovering, he chased 13 ships in the French Fleet to Egypt and found them anchored at the mouth of the Nile. He systematically destroyed the French fleet and the decisive Battle of the Nile delivered his title of Baron. He returned to Naples for repairs – and for his lover – who stage managed a hero's welcome, organising a dukedom of Bronte in Sicily. Nelson openly disobeyed orders to sail to Minorca. The Admiralty ordered him home to modify his behaviour and bravado – not least with Mrs Hamilton – whom he accompanied, with her husband in tow! His arrival was greeted with a triumphal procession to London and faced with his popularity, the Admiralty promoted him to Vice Admiral. Emma Hamilton's pregnancy was uncomfortable but ignored.

British tactics were now to harass potential enemies and weaken Bonaparte's position on land. Nelson sailed to Copenhagen and won a resounding victory against the Danes, his trademark personal risk and superbly trained crews, carrying the day. Bonaparte was preparing for an invasion of England and Nelson chased the French squadrons through the Western Mediterranean and made

dispositions for the blockade of Cadiz. In England, Nelson planned his campaign in the face of Bonaparte's invasion, he seemed the only hope of salvation for the British.

Bonaparte ordered his fleets to break the blockade and the Franco-Spanish fleets were sighted off Cape Trafalgar. As the fleets engaged, Nelson gave his signal that he 'hoped every man would do his duty'. Battle raged around Nelson's flagship, *HMS Victory*. The English had taken 15 ships, however Nelson was felled by a French sniper. As he lay dying, he spoke to Thomas Hardy, saying he hoped that they would take 20 and that, 'I have done my duty' (many other versions exist of his final words). England had been saved, but the mourning for Nelson overshadowed the victory. His majestic funeral and his tomb in St Paul's Cathedral are testament to the love bestowed on him.

That love did not extend to Emma Hamilton, who died destitute in Calais nine years later. Her daughter by Nelson, Horatia, ironically married a clergyman in Norfolk and raised a large family.

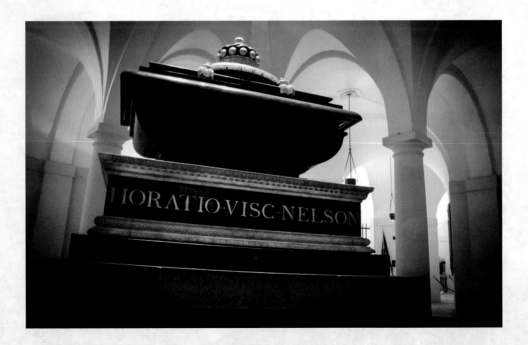

Horatio Nelson

NAPOLEON BONAPARTE
(1769–1821)

LES INVALIDES, PARIS, FRANCE

More than the Revolution itself, Napoleon reshaped and redefined Europe. The move from medieval absolutism to a sense of the modern and democratic was carried on the shoulders of a military dictator rather than on the high flown moral notions of liberty and democracy.

Napoleon Bonaparte was born on August 15, 1769 to a moderately wealthy aristocratic Italian family in Corsica, which was then under French rule. Educational options were limited in Corsica and Napoleon undertook studies in mainland France, firstly at Autun and then, at a military academy in Brienne-le-Château. He finally completed his studies in Paris at École Militaire, graduating in 1785. Bonaparte was at once swept up in activities of the French Revolution and, as a fervent Corsican Nationalist, he agitated for Corsican independence. His actions in supporting the Revolution at the siege of Toulon had him promoted to Brigadier General at age 24 in command of the French Army. His strategic genius recognised, he was increasingly relied upon to repel British actions against the fledgling Republic which brought him sudden wealth and fame.

It was his military career outside of France that secured Bonaparte's reputation, particularly in the Italian campaign where he defeated the Austrian armies and ended Venetian independence after 1100 years. In an attempt to weaken British influence, Bonaparte attacked Egypt. In his absence, the Republic began to weaken in popularity and on his return in 1799 Bonaparte overthrew the government and established himself as consul and then Emperor (1804). In doing so, he had emulated his hero, Caesar.

It was from this point that Europe was plunged into a series of destructive and destabilising wars that lasted another decade. Napoleon struck east against the Austrians, his victories described in military terms as classic, brought an end the Holy Roman Empire, an institution of eastern Europe that had lasted for 800 years. Coalitions of empires and nations had little effect on Napoleon's successes until he thrust into Russia and was rebuffed by the winter (10,000 men were lost to the cold on the night of 8–9 November) and the extraordinary scorched earth policy, saw Moscow burn rather than surrender. Napoleon's retreat enthused opposition, and led by the British, Prussia and Austria, Napoleon was defeated on the field in the Battle of Leipzig (1813). Napoleon's generals eventually mutinied on April 6, 1814 Napoleon abdicated and was sent to Elba, an island off the Tuscan coast where he had sovereignty. Barely eight months later, he returned to France after escaping, faced down his army and challenging them to kill him, whereby they responded with *"Vive L'Empereur"*. Napoleon rallied 200,000 men to his cause and drove on to attack the British and Prussian forces at Waterloo. He was crushed and fled to claim asylum from a British captain.

He was sent to Saint Helena in the Atlantic Ocean, 1870 kilometres from Africa's west coast where he was supervised by British captors and treated with suspicion and harshness. By 1821, Napoleon's health had deteriorated and he died on May 5, 1821. He was interred on the island.

In 1840 Louis-Philippe, King of France, demanded the return of the Emperor's remains and the central crypt of the Église du Dôme Church in the Les Invalides was prepared for his burial which took place 21 years later on completion. His remains are protected by six concentric coffins and entombed in a magnificent porphyry sarcophagus, on a green granite plinth surrounded by the emblems of

the territories he conquered.

Napoleon has been characterised as a megalomaniac, narcissist and dictator however his legacy is of a Eurocentric world, a rejection of the absolutism of the past and a lover of the actions of the revolution. He was the man of the age – to create a new world an old one must be torn apart – this was Napoleon's legacy. Napoleon's military genius shook worlds, and the ideals of the revolution passed into mainstream thought from his time onwards.

Napoleon Bonaparte

ABRAHAM LINCOLN
(1809–1865)

OAK RIDGE CEMETERY,
SPRINGFIELD, ILLINOIS, USA

More than any other US President, Abraham Lincoln is identified with the essence of his nation. Today, he is regarded more highly than any other American President in history and yet his fate was tied to that other American penchant – the assassination of their leaders, and the invisible divisions that still exist in the nation.

Lincoln embodied the traits that Americans identify as worthy – individual, self-made, moral and self-reliant. Lincoln grew up on the western frontier, in Kentucky and Illinois, in a strict Baptist family stamped with high moral standards and a particular disregard for slavery, at this time the mainstay for wealth in the States. Ironically, he married Mary Todd whose family were very wealthy slave traders in Lexington.

Self-taught as a lawyer, Lincoln developed an interest in politics after a failed attempt in business and was admitted to the bar in 1836. After a very successful legal and State political career his cause célèbre was slavery, which he regarded as a scourge, and creating a 'house divided' in the nation.

It was on this cause, along with a program of reforming economic policies that Lincoln ran for president in 1860. He was elected 16th President of the US but his support was isolated in the North and West and the slave states of the South moved to leave the Union before his inauguration. En route to his inauguration several assassination plots were foiled by his security, Allan Pinkerton. His inaugural address confirmed that he had no intention to 'interfere' with slavery yet the Secessionist movement and Lincoln's refusal to accept the destruction of the Union led to the bloody Civil War. When Confederate forces fired on Union troops at Fort Sumter on April 12, 1861, the war had begun.

Lincoln took on his role as Commander in Chief, expanded legal powers of arrest of sympathisers, introduced a draft and ran a relentless and bloody war to destroy Confederate economic power, his enemys' army and liberate southern slaves. These strategies as well as the decisive and brutal leadership of Ulysses S. Grant delivered victory after four years when the Confederate General Lee surrendered on April 6, 1865.

Lincoln won his second term in 1865 and set about reconstruction but his plans were cut short by John Wilkes Booth. A well-known actor and Confederate spy, Booth conceived of a plan to kidnap Lincoln and demand the release of Confederate prisoners.

Abraham Lincoln

However, after hearing Lincoln's speech promoting voting rights for former slaves, Booth was incensed and planned to kill both Lincoln and Grant at the Ford Theatre and to have the vice president killed in his home. Grant changed his plans and did not attend the theatre. While Lincoln's bodyguard was drinking in a saloon at 10.13 pm, Booth crept up behind Lincoln as the President watched the play *Our American Cousin* and shot him in the back of the skull. Lincoln died the next morning on April 15, 1865; Booth escaped and was shot on April 26, 1865.

Lincoln's flag enfolded body was taken to the White House and lay in state until April 21. He was then transported to a magnificent funerary train that wound its way back through the Northern states to Springfield, Illinois. Lincoln's body lies entombed in the Oak Ridge Cemetery, a magnificent 36-metre obelisk and mausoleum. The tomb was reconstructed many times and Lincoln's body has 'survived' bomb threats and a kidnapping, and been moved 17 times and viewed five times. The president is honoured by the Lincoln Memorial in Washington DC.

Perhaps there has never been a man that so symbolised all that it is to be American.

GEORGE ARMSTRONG CUSTER
(1839–1876)

WEST POINT CEMETERY, NEW YORK, USA

No more controversial figure of his time, no more committed to fame and no more egotistical. General George Armstrong Custer consolidated his place in American folklore with his death and that of his command at the Battle of the Little Big Born in the Indian Wars in 1876.

Custer was born in Rumley, Ohio but spent much of his early life in Michigan. He entered West Point in 1858, but graduated out as part of the class of 1862, prompted by the beginning of the Civil War. A terrible student, Custer graduated last, primarily for disciplinary reasons, and in a sense the Civil War saved him. He joined his regiment at the battle of Bull Run. He began to ingratiate himself with superiors (a tactic he employed throughout his military life) and won over General Pleasonton in the Gettysburg campaign with his willingness to lead attacks. Pleasonton promoted him to Brigadier General of Volunteers at the age of 23. The 'boy General' won attention from the press with his dashing but reckless style. It was his success in breaking the Confederate forces at East Cavalry Field that won him renown,

despite the cost of 257 men (the highest loss of any cavalry brigade). Custer went on to greater successes at Petersburg and the defeat of the Confederate General, Jubal Early. By the end of the war he had established himself as a maverick force in the Army and in the public's imagination.

The end of the war saw Custer at a loss. He had married well and now sought not only the fame he was obsessed with but also the wealth. He considered a post as general in the army of Benito Juarez in Mexico and running for Congress and accepted a tour support of President Johnson of the South. He was then appointed lieutenant colonel of the 7th Cavalry in Kansas in the expedition against the Plains Indians, a decision that would establish his notoriety.

He established Camp Supply in November 1868 and led the subsequent attack against the Cheyenne at the battle of the Washita River. According to his accounts, 103 warriors were killed and 53 women and children were captured. This attack forced a substantial number of Cheyenne people into reservations, which opened up the Black Hills for gold prospecting – the policy base for the wars. The gold rush and corruption scandals that followed dragged President Grant's brother into controversy. Custer was writing magazine articles criticising the President and his peace policy and Custer became embroiled in a long running dispute with the President and narrowly avoided arrest. His writing and exploits had endeared him to the public and Grant relented in his arrest and set a deadline for the solution of the Indian problem.

The Lakota holy man, Sitting Bull, had called together the largest ever gathering of Plains Indians at Ash Creek but had moved the meeting to the Little Big Horn River. This was reported to Custer by Crow scouts on June 25 and Custer, supported by Marcus Reno and Frederick Benteen divided his forces to attack from the north, south and east of the encampment. Reno's charge failed and stalled and he was forced to retreat into bluffs above the river, effectively taking him from battle. Custer had attacked from the north but was outflanked by Crazy Horse and his warriors to his north and above Custer on a ridge. Crazy Horse and White Bull led a charge that broke Custer's diminished line and he took his 'last stand' on a knoll with about 40 other cavalry. The warriors rode them down with lances. Custer's men had shot their horses to use them as cover and the warriors killed every man in the command.

Custer's death is shrouded in uncertainty, exacerbated by Cheyenne silence, contradictory accounts and battlefield chaos. He suffered two fatal wounds, one to his left temple and one above the heart. His younger brothers had died with him at Little Big Horn. General Terry arrived two days later and found most of the bodies scalped and mutilated. Custer's body was buried on the battlefield and his remains returned to West Point Cemetery on October 10, 1877. The battle site was designated a national Cemetery in 1976.

His death had brought him the fame that he had desperately sought in life. His wife's extensive writings about his campaigns, his flirtation with the press and his flamboyant disregard for others has cast him as a deluded narcissist or foolhardy adventurer-hero. A Cheyenne sharpshooter ended that adventure, that day.

George Armstrong Custer

LOUIS PASTEUR
(1822–1895)

CATHEDRAL OF NOTRE DAME (MEMORIAL AND TOMB), LATER INTERRED PASTEUR INSTITUTE, PARIS, FRANCE

A young boy whose academic ability teetered on the edge of average was driven by personal tragedy to become the most eminent biological scientist of his age. Pasteur saved the lives of millions, courted controversy and earned his place in Notre Dame as a hero of a different kind.

The son of a poor tanner, Louis Pasteur was the third child of Jean Pasteur and Jeanne Roqui and was born on December 27, 1822 in Dole, France. Louis left home to study in Paris in 1839 but returned, homesick and disillusioned. He had developed an interest in science, eventually passing his baccalauréat scientifique (although with a poor grade in chemistry) and pursued a variety of degrees. He finally became a professor of chemistry at the University of Strasbourg in 1848. Pasteur courted and married the Rector's daughter, Marie Laurent, and went on to have five children together, three of whom were killed by typhoid.

These tragedies shaped the rest of Pasteur's life.

Having moved to Lille University and then to Paris, Pasteur began his investigation of infection, which led him to establish the Pasteur Institute. He reshaped the scientific method with stricter emphasis on observation rather than speculation. Through observation he developed germ theory – the idea that germs enter a body and cause disease, rather than the idea of 'spontaneous generation' – and applied this to work on beer, milk and wine. His experiments with heat stopping the 'spoiling' of liquids transformed public health and survival rates in infants changed dramatically based on Pasteur's work.

His work on immunology, discovered through an accident, showed that mild exposure to a disease (chicken cholera) could be used as a means of vaccination. A batch of chickens had survived the exposure, and although assumed to be a mistake by his assistant Chamberland, however, Pasteur theorised the correct answer. He applied the method to anthrax and eventually rabies, applying his vaccine to nine-year-old Joseph Meister, who had been mauled by a rabid dog,

Louis Pasteur

and saved him.

From 1868, Pasteur suffered a series of strokes, but he continued with his work with his notorious fearlessness (he once took saliva from a rabid bulldog's mouth, flouting legal boundaries as he was not a licensed doctor). He protected himself from infection by washing his hands, and encouraging surgeons to do the same (few doctors took the precaution until Pasteur's work).

Pasteur's health was compromised by another stroke in 1894 from which he failed to fully recover and he died in 1895 in Paris. Already declared a national hero by 1878, by age 55 Pasteur had won ten prestigious national and international awards. He was buried in Notre Dame Cathedral and was later interred in a crypt at the Pasteur Institute.

Strangely, in 1878, Pasteur had instructed his family to never release his laboratory notes. These stayed secret until 1971 when they were released under catalogue numbers in the Bibliothèque National. His notes reveal his personality – dogmatic, renegade, arrogant, unfair and unflinching. These were the aspects of himself that he wanted hidden – along with his renewed Catholic faith which he had deserted so long ago in response to the mysterious deaths of three of his children. Pasteur relentlessly sought the answer to this mystery and solved it, saving the lives of millions of infants.

LAWRENCE OF ARABIA (1888–1935)

CHURCH OF ST. NICHOLAS AND ST. MAGNUS, MORETON, ENGLAND

The desire for an unremarkable life, a veiled existence serving the downtrodden in a foreign land whose stark loneliness and quiet held sway over the imagination – was denied to the gentleman adventurer who was Lawrence of Arabia.

Thomas Edward Lawrence, the second of five sons, was born out of wedlock on August 16, 1888, to Sir Thomas Chapman and Sarah Junner. Chapman had left his wife and first family in Ireland to live with Junner, and they called themselves Mr and Mrs Lawrence. The family settled in Wales, where Thomas Edward (known as Ned) was born and after some restlessness the Lawrence family finally settled in Oxford in 1896 where Thomas Edward was educated. Though highly literate, his interests were for the outdoors, adventure and history. At age 15 he and friend Cyril Beeson cycled three counties and recorded monuments and antiquities, repeating these efforts in 1906 and 1907 in France. Lawrence then entered Jesus College, Oxford.

In 1909 Lawrence undertook a solo walking tour of 1000 miles (1600 kilometres) in Ottoman, Syria. After the completion of his degree he began work as a practising archaeologist at Carchemish near Baghdad. His fluency in Arabic, French and Ancient Greek was invaluable. Lawrence and fellow archaeologist Leonard Wooley, were co-opted by the British Government to undertake an archaeological survey of the Negev Desert, a smokescreen for intelligence work. Lawrence's intimacy with the Ottoman Empire led to his posting to Cairo after hostilities began in 1914.

British Intelligence plans were to create insurgency in the Ottoman Empire and Lawrence was perfectly suited. Described as loyal, with steely bravery, Lawrence was sent to direct the campaign in 1916, using the Arab tribal irregulars to destroy and disrupt railways and fortresses. Lawrence was completely trusted by the Arab tribes and his ingenuity in strategy and ruthless self-sacrifice led to victories throughout the Arabian Peninsula. He led the once divided tribes to victories in Yanbu, Medina, Aqaba, and Tafileh and eventually into Damascus.

His exploits were recorded by war correspondent Lowell Thomas who followed Lawrence in 1918. Lawrence's appearance in Bedouin clothing, and the brutal realities of guerrilla war were romanticised by Thomas in a series of lectures and films. Lawrence had become a media sensation, a burden he was to carry uncomfortably for the remainder of his life.

After 1918, the realities of post war diplomacy shook Lawrence's faith in his wartime masters, particularly Churchill. He had promised the Arabs freedom but instead the power brokers of Europe oversaw the establishment of new influence and control. After his experiences at the Peace Conferences, Lawrence returned to London a disillusioned hero, coveted and adored but seeking anonymity. He, ironically, attempted to hide behind false identities, much like his father, and enlisted in the RAF as 'John Hume Ross' but was identified. He enlisted in the Tank Corps but unhappy there, he applied again to the RAF and was sent to remote India as a spy. He returned in 1928.

A fresh surge of popularity came with the publication of his *Seven Pillars of Wisdom*, a detailed account of his campaigns, military strategy and geography, and then *Revolt in the Desert*, which was an abridged account, with renewed lectures and tours by Lowell. This brought wealth (eventually) to Lawrence but he

craved a secret, quiet life at his simple house in Chingford. The publications had brought into question his personal life. Guarded and secretive always, Lawrence's only associations seem to have been homosexual but there is no direct evidence of any sexual liaisons and some biographers have suggested he was asexual.

He continued to serve in the RAF until 1935. At age 46, while indulging in his hobby of riding powerful motorbikes, his Brough Superior SS100 hit a dip in the road which obscured his view of two boys cycling. He swerved and crashed. He died six days later on May 19, 1935.

It has been suggested that his life was a tragic reflection of the times. Lawrence was a disillusioned modern hero; complex and distant, unknowable, exposed to brutal realities that he faced with heroism and misunderstanding. He was, though, a truly remarkable man – his name (a media construction) ever associated a place he knew, loved and in a sense, betrayed.

Lawrence of Arabia

OSKAR SCHINDLER
(1908–1974)

MOUNT ZION ROMAN
CATHOLIC FRANCISCAN
CEMETERY, JERUSALEM, ISRAEL

Industrialist, profiteer, spy, black marketeer, Nazi and saviour. There was no more unlikely a man to be considered 'Righteous among the nations', the highest accolade bestowed upon non-Jews, than a womanising alcoholic for his services in saving 1200 Jews from extermination in the gas chambers.

Oskar Schindler was born in Moravia on April 28, 1908 in Czechoslovakia. An ethnic German and part of the Sudeten Germans, Schindler had an unremarkable childhood. Enrolled in a technical high school, Schindler worked for his father's farm machinery business until meeting Emelie Pelzl whom he married. The young couple lived with Oskar's parents for seven years until the family business failed and Schindler found employment with the Bank of Prague between 1931 and 1938. This bland existence disguised Schindler's other life; he was a member of the German Sudeten Party from 1935 and a Nazi Abwehr spy from 1936. He funnelled information to the Nazi's about Czech railway and military installations and was arrested in 1938 but released

under the Munich Agreement. After being promoted in the Abwehr, he was sent to the Czech-Polish border in 1939 to collect information in the lead-up to the German invasion of Poland.

Schindler arrived in Krakow in October 1939, and he quickly made contacts both in the black market and with Jews who were newly dispossessed of property and businesses. Schindler took over one of these businesses and renamed it Deutsche Emaillewaren-Frabrik, to manufacture cookware for the Wehrmacht and SS. Jews secretly financed his lease and his contracts with the German forces were consolidated with bribes.

He lived the lifestyle of a profiteer; lavish and excessive, affairs and drunkenness de rigueur. His wife moved to Krakow to control his behaviour and initially he had no interest in helping dispossessed Jews. He was primarily concerned with having his factories classified as essential to the war effort and thereby, protected.

His witnessing of the 'aktion', the liquidation of the Krakow Ghetto and the establishment of Plaszów concentration camp along with the brutality employed by the Nazis was a revelation for Schindler. From March 13, 1943 onwards he worked to protect his Jewish workers from extermination. Plaszów concentration camp was run by the psychopathic Amon Goeth. Schindler convinced Goeth (through bribery and flattery) to allow him to build a camp to house his workers, making them safe from Goeth's arbitrary murders. Schindler had been arrested several times by the Nazi authorities, largely to put upward pressure on his bribes and assert their power. As the Red Army pushed through Eastern Europe the SS tightened the reins and began shifting Nazi possessions west for security – and exterminating the 'Jewish Problem'. Schindler had his factory reclassified as a grenade production facility and the workers and the factories were relocated in 1944 to Brunnlitz in Czechoslovakia. The famous list was generated for this move. Several times during the move, when workers were accidently moved to Auschwitz, Schindler negotiated their return.

In the new factory SS guards, Schindler, Emilie and the workers listened to Churchill's speech announcing the German surrender on May 7, 1945.

Schindler and Emilie escaped west to Switzerland, with the assistance of American Jewish officers.

Oskar Schindler

Schindler spent his remaining years in failed businesses in Argentina and West Germany. The American Jewish Committee paid him compensation of $15,000. It was estimated he spent over a million dollars to bribe SS and other officials to save his Jews. He described his actions, 'I felt the Jews were being destroyed. I had to help them. There was no choice.'

A man enlightened by experience, who discovered his humanity in the most extreme circumstances, Schindler's grave is honoured in Jerusalem's Mount Zion Catholic Cemetery, covered in pebbles, symbolic of the numbers on the list. He is the only member of the Nazi Party to be buried in Israel.

Oskar Schindler

Chapter Four

POPULAR
MUSIC

BUDDY HOLLY
(1936–1959)

CITY OF LUBBOCK CEMETERY,
LUBBOCK, TEXAS, USA

Rock and roll pioneer, innovator and Texan gentleman, Charles Hardin 'Buddy' Holley was born on September 7, 1936 in Lubbock, Texas. The youngest of three brothers, Buddy was taught to play guitar and banjo by his elder brothers but his singing came naturally. At age five he won a talent contest and at 13 recorded Hank Snow's blues classic 'My Two Timin Woman' in his soprano voice. His musical abilities shone at school and he began performing with school friend Robert Montgomery as 'Buddy and Bob' at the local bluegrass station KDAV and at talent shows.

Ambitious, talented and adept, Holly took direction from acts that toured including Elvis Presley and Bill Haley and the rockabilly style that came from Sun Records. Holly, Montgomery and Larry Welborn opened for Elvis in Lubbock in 1955, catching the eye of Decca Record scouts and he was signed in February 1956. The record company misspelt his birth name. He formed his own band named the Crickets and went to Nashville to record with Owen Bradley.

Holly was unhappy with his input and the control of Bradley in the session and the two singles 'Blue Days, Black nights' and 'Modern Don Juan' went nowhere. During the sessions, a ballad version of 'That'll be the Day' was cut but never released. Just as quickly, Holly was released from his contract to record with other labels. Holly realised he needed a manager that could control his output and hired Norman Petty and began recording at Petty's New Mexico studio. He and the band were soon signed to Brunswick Records. Holly also signed as a solo artist with Coral Records – an unusual position then, but de rigueur in the industry from the seventies. In effect, he was operating two careers at once.

'That'll be the Day' (the title taken from John Wayne's dialogue in the 1956 classic, *The Searchers*) was released on May 27, 1957. The song, now upbeat and defined as rock and roll, hit No.1 in the US and Britain, and Holly and the Crickets appeared on *The Ed Sullivan Show*, an acknowledgement they had truly 'arrived'. The hit 'Peggy Sue' followed, and debut albums were released in the following February. Holly appeared on all the music mainstays and toured widely, including black clubs like the Apollo in New York. It was Holly's increasing interest in New York that saw the Crickets split in 1958 and Holly go on to explore the diverse music on offer in the City. He was particularly interested in collaborations with Ray Charles and Mahalia Jackson and wanted to branch into film.

The roller coaster continued with his love life; he proposed to his wife María Santiago on their first date. She spoke of true love at first sight and the couple married less than two months later. They set up in Greenwich Village where Holly recorded his acoustic album *Apartment Tapes,* but the roller coaster faltered. Norman Perry had been funnelling royalties into his company and despite his enormous success, Holly was forced back out on the road to pay for rent and to support his pregnant wife.

Following a performance in Iowa, Holly chartered a small plane and took Richie Valens and JP Richardson (the Big Bopper) to the next town – the pilot and all on board were killed. The bodies lay in the February snow all night. Waylon Jennings had joked that he hoped the plane would crash, teasing Holly about how he and the support band were following by bus. Jennings was haunted by his comment for decades.

Holly lies in the City of Lubbock Cemetery, his headstone simply has his name correctly spelt ('Holley') and a carving of his trademark Fender Stratocaster. His wife María did not attend the funeral and has never visited the gravesite. She blamed her pregnancy for forcing Buddy back on the road. She miscarried the day after his death.

BRIAN JONES
(1942–1969)

CHELTENHAM CEMETERY,
CHELTENHAM, ENGLAND

Lewis Brian Hopkins Jones was the founding member of the Rolling Stones and the first of the '27 Club' of rock stars to die at the age of 27. Jones was born in 1942 to middle class parents in Cheltenham, Gloucestershire, both of whom had strong interests and abilities in music. He attended local schools and was a gifted academic student (an IQ of 135) but with a rebellious attitude that rejected the conformity of schooling.

His passions became blues music, particularly that of Elmore James (his own pseudonym was Elmore Lewis) and women. He had fathered five children to a variety of young women by the age of 23. He was a gifted multi-instrumentalist, playing keyboards, guitar and harp. He moved to London to establish himself in the nascent blues scene, and established contact with Alexis Korner, the blues powerhouse.

He was obsessed with forming a credible blues outfit and advertised in *Jazz News* for musicians to audition at the Bricklayer's Arms on May 2, 1962.

Ian Stewart, a piano player, was the first to respond. Mick Jagger appeared later and brought his childhood friend Keith Richards, and the hub of the Rolling Stones (named by Jones) was born. Wyman and Watts joined later. The band, ostensibly led by Jones, began a busy recording and gigging schedule with hits in the blues vein, but the power structure in the band began to shift as Jagger and Richards formed their writing partnership and began to deliver original hits.

Jones' inability to write songs and his increasing drug and alcohol abuse began to distance him from the band, his manipulative and manic behaviour alienated those closest to him. Jones was failing to function and his playing suffered. The success that manager Andrew Loog-Oldham created for the band, along with Jones' girlfriend, Anita Pallenberg, leaving him for Keith Richards, drove not just a rift but a chasm between the two elements of the Rolling Stones. He was unable to make sessions and when the Stones decided to tour the US for the first time in three years it was decided that he must leave. Jagger, Richards and Watts delivered the news to him on June 8, 1969. Jones was resident at Cotchford Farm during this time of alienation, a place of indulgence and isolation that allowed Jones to experiment with LSD, cocaine and methamphetamines. His appearance became more unorthodox and his then girlfriend, Anna Wohlin, spoke of times she spent dressing and making him up. Such was the musical driving force now – narcissistic and withdrawn.

At midnight on July 2, 1969 Jones was found motionless at the bottom of his swimming pool at Cotchford Farm. Wohlin maintained that he had a pulse but had expired by the time doctors had arrived. The autopsy and coroner's report stated 'death by misadventure', his liver and heart enlarged by drug use and a lifelong asthmatic condition. Conspiracy theories emerged immediately, some suggesting that Richards was somehow involved, that a tradesman murdered him for money and that documents were being burnt at 7am by people unknown.

Bizarrely Jones' body was buried three metres deep, his hair bleached white and placed in an airtight metal casket to deter trophy hunters. The Stones played a free concert in Hyde Park two days after Jones' death. Jagger quoted Shelley and butterflies were released in memoriam but the reality was the concert was to introduce Mick Taylor, the Stones new guitarist to the world. They had moved on.

Brian Jones

'Influential...important...intelligent – but just wasted it', so Bill Wyman encapsulates Jones. The quiet Stone said so much.

Brian Jones

JIMI HENDRIX
(1942–1970)

GREENWOOD MEMORIAL PARK,
RENTON, WASHINGTON, USA

Hendrix defined a generation, embodying the ideals of 'hippiedom' his magical reinvention of the electric guitar with his definitive performance at Woodstock. His death reflects a young man paying the price and reaping the rewards of the ephemeral life of a rock god. Born James Marshall Hendrix in Seattle, Washington, Hendrix's early life was dishevelled. His parents, both alcoholics, argued violently and frequently, forcing the young Jimmy to hide in cupboards to avoid injury and was often sent to his grandmother's in Vancouver as respite. A sensitive young boy, his early life experiences haunted him. His parents divorced and his father, Al, was given custody of Jimi and his older brother, Leon. It was while working with his father that he discovered a ukulele and was able to pick out melodies almost immediately. His first guitar came a year later, costing five dollars.

He quickly became adept and started his first band, the Velvetones with school friends from Washington Junior High. His virtuosity annoyed early band members

and he was often fired, a trait that followed him in his early sideman years with Little Richard and The Isley Brothers. Some stability came into his existence when he enlisted in the army (an option he took rather than prison for being involved with stolen cars). Despite later rumours of injury, he was honourably discharged on the basis of unsuitability; his obsession with the guitar now dominated his existence.

He moved to Nashville to establish himself on the 'chitlin' circuit', playing for a range of soul, R&B and blues musicians (notably Sam Cooke and Wilson Pickett), his first recordings appear in 1964 with The Isley Brothers and Little Richard. The restrictions of sideman and session roles frustrated Hendrix and he moved to Greenwich Village where he picked up a residency at Café Wha. Linda Keith, Keith Richards then girlfriend, saw Hendrix and introduced him to a range of managers. Chas Chandler, late bassist of The Animals, saw Hendrix performing a cover of 'Hey Joe', was stunned and negotiated a contract and brought him to London. His performances impressed the music elite; Jeff Beck commenting that 'he would have to find something else to do.' His musicianship and virtuosity redefined how the electric guitar functioned in music. He blistered up the UK charts and began compiling material for an LP release between performances.

Hendrix's career functioned around signature live performances; blazing guitar, literally, at Monterey Pop 1967, Bill Graham's Fillmore 5 night extravaganza and finally at Woodstock. His rendition of 'Star Spangled Banner' snatched the sixties zeitgeist. Between these moments Hendrix's album performances are similarly astonishing, *Axis: Bold as Love* and *Electric Ladyland* were described as the apex of individual performance by a musician in rock; wide ranging in appeal and style.

Hendrix's other obsession started to impact his existence. The Jimi Hendrix Experience began to break up as Hendrix's use of drugs and alcohol began to escalate. Hendrix's performances became erratic and he searched for new musical combinations with the Band of Gypsies and Cry of Love band. His performance came to crisis point on the European leg of the Cry of Love tour, abandoning playing after two or three songs and being booed off stage in Germany, incapable of playing through an LSD trip. Hendrix had been arrested for possession of heroin and cannabis in Toronto in 1969, and it weighed heavily on his mind while awaiting

trial. He was acquitted but the arrest pointed to the seriousness of his problem, and within a year he was dead. Hendrix and his girlfriend, Monika Dannemann spent the last hours of his life together at the Samarkand Hotel in London. She prepared a late meal; they shared a bottle of wine, she drove to the residence of an acquaintance, picked him up again at 3am and returned to sleep. When she awoke Hendrix was breathing but unresponsive, and he was pronounced dead at 12:45pm on September 18, 1970. An autopsy showed he had ingested 18 times the recommended dose of barbiturates – Dannemann's prescribed sleeping tablets.

Hendrix's body was flown to Seattle to lay with his mother, and more than 200 people attended the funeral.

Hendrix's legacy is vibrant – the many contracts he signed allowed posthumous release of material and there is not a young guitar player that has not appreciated the majesty of his Fender Stratocaster.

Jimi Hendrix

JIM MORRISON
(1943–1971)

Père Lachaise Cemetery, Paris, France

An icon of the sixties counter culture, James Douglas 'Jim' Morrison was born in Melbourne, Florida on December 8, 1943. His father was a naval officer and so the Morrison family moved often and consequently the young James was constantly adjusting to new friends and new situations. Jim withdrew into the world of literature at an early age and impressed his teachers with a vast array of reading and knowledge, focusing on Nietzsche, Rimbaud, Kafka and Cocteau. He eventually graduated from Florida State University but went on to attend UCLA's film school within the Theatre Arts department of the College of Fine Arts.

His time at film school led him to Venice Beach and to meeting Ray Manzarek, another film school graduate who became the crux of The Doors. Manzarek was impressed with Morrison's lyrics and obsessed with their poetic form. Auditions brought John Densmore on drums and blues guitarist Robbie Krieger. Morrison played no instruments and he was assumed to write the lyrics, but many of The Doors' hits were actually written by Krieger. It was on stage that Morrison made

his most significant contribution to the band.

Morrison often extemporised over jams, and it was this and his recklessness on stage (famously being charged with indecent exposure in stage in Miami) and in life that stamped him as a favourite of Californian counter culture. The Doors signed with Electra in 1967 and 'Light my Fire' stayed three weeks at Number 1 on the charts. By the time of their second album they were one of the most popular bands in the US. The music was supplemented by images of Morrison, most famously 'The Young Lion' semi-nude shots that were released in 1967. These cemented Morrison as a sex symbol and rock god.

In typical hippie style, however, Morrison's life began to spiral out of control as the band's popularity skyrocketed. The albums *Morrison Hotel* and *L.A. Woman* were massive hits but Morrison's heavy drinking and use of LSD had bloated his once svelte body and now he hid behind a large beard. He had cut contact with his family, and falsely claimed that his parents and siblings were dead. He spoke often of a fundamental turning point of seeing a dying Native American in a road accident as a child that was dismissed by his family but became his point of separation from them. His relationship with long-time companion Pamela Courson also became unstable. Their open relationship caused friction, as did their increasing use of cocaine and heroin. Jim's frequent associations with groupies saw three paternity actions filed against him at the time of his death.

Courson and Morrison had withdrawn to Paris in early 1971 and Morrison tried to reshape himself and his image, losing weight and the beard. He died on July 3, 1971, found in a bathtub on the Rue Beautreillis. He was 27.

There were many questions over the nature of his death. No autopsy was performed because the French police found no evidence of foul play. Morrison is said to have inhaled Courson's heroin, mistakenly thinking it was cocaine and haemorrhaged to death in his bath. Witnesses claim that Morrison's burial in Père Lachaise was a pitiful affair, with only several mourners and a few bouquets hastily thrown on the casket, leading to some speculation that Morrison had faked his death.

Morrison's grave is one of the most frequently visited in Père Lachasie but it had no official marker until French authorities placed a shield marker which was stolen in 1973. Croatian sculptor Mikulin placed a bust of his own design on the grave that was systematically defaced and finally stolen in 1988. Morrison's estranged father placed a flat stone bearing the quote, 'True to himself' in Greek (the translation of the inscription actually says, 'according to his own daemon'). It was an acknowledgement perhaps to Morrison's pursuit of the ideal and the duality of human existence.

Jim Morrison

ELVIS PRESLEY
(1935–1977)

GRACELAND MANSION ESTATES, MEMPHIS, TENNESSEE, USA

If American popular culture is defined by its dominance of the entertainment industry, then Elvis Presley defines dominance of the generation of rock and roll. His grave has become part of the iconography of the South, popularised in song it is the place of pilgrimage for those who idolise the man, his music and the representation he gave to the generation of 'rock and roll'.

Elvis Aaron Presley was born in Tupelo, Mississippi, the second of twins, his older brother was stillborn. Presley's family were part of the urban, white, poor of the South. His father unambitious, his mother took strength from religion and the family was often assisted by the State or family members to survive. As a child Presley showed some ability in singing but stage fright crippled his performance to a large extent.

After a move to Memphis, Tennessee, Presley's interest in music was heightened by exposure to rockabilly rather than the southern gospel that dominated at home. Considered to be from a 'trashy' home and bullied at times at school, young Elvis'

singing ability, a performance on an annual 'Minstrel' show, saw his popularity change and confirmed his own ambition to make it in music. Ironically, music was the only subject he failed in school.

In August 1953 Elvis went to Sun Records to cut tracks but his debut failed to impress, until he was teamed with Scotty Moore and Bill Black. In a pre-session jam, Elvis sang 'That's all Right', complete with gyrations and posing. Black joined in and Sam Phillips, producer and owner of Sun, recorded the song. The single was followed up with live performances and Elvis quickly became a regional star. His stage performances were riveting and regular TV appearances on *Louisiana Hayride* brought him to the attention of Colonel Tom Parker. Further sessions produced 'Heartbreak Hotel' and 'Blue Suede Shoes' and Elvis' self-titled album showcased guitar rather than piano. 'Rock and Roll' became an entity – and that entity was embodied in Elvis Presley.

Mainstream entertainment vilified Elvis, the gyrations and the black influence in his music alienated the industry but the necessity of TV exposure meant that Elvis would need to compromise. His performances on *The Ed Sullivan Show*, photographed from waist up to curtail his sexuality, actually galvanised his stardom. This success (a million advance orders for 'Love Me Tender') brought Elvis into the mainstream.

In this dizzy rush of stardom, however, the Memphis Draft Board called Elvis to the army.

Presley served in the army from 1958 to 1960; during this time his beloved mother died, he met his future wife (then 14-year-old) Priscilla Beaulieu whilst stationed in Germany and developed an addiction to amphetamines. Convinced that his draft had ended his career, on discharge Elvis conceded to Parker's demands that he focus on his film career and accompanying soundtrack music to re-establish his pop profile. This led to a string of B-grade films, a waning in the quality of recorded material and no live performances for seven years. Elvis had become mainstream, lost in the blandness of Hollywood.

His return to the stage came in 1968 with a TV special and although proving his genuine performance skill, the world had moved on. His choice of material was divorced from current tastes and the burgeoning counterculture saw Elvis

Elvis Presley

as a parody of his earlier career. In concert and in life, Elvis portrayed his pro-US, conservative politics, emphasised by his association with US President Nixon. A long running residency in Las Vegas confirmed this shift where his stage clothing became increasingly enormous karate style pyjamas.

Presley's marriage began to breakdown, coinciding with his growing reliance on barbiturates. Later performances saw him almost incoherent and concerts were truncated and embarrassing; he had become a caricature of the man that had reshaped American culture.

On August 16, 1977, Presley was found unresponsive on the bathroom floor at Graceland; the cause of death uncertain but autopsy details implicate many medical conditions, including heart disease, all aggravated or possibly caused by drug abuse.

Thousands viewed the open casket at Graceland and 80,000 lined the processional route to Forest Hill where Elvis was buried next to his mother. Following attempts to steal the body, both remains were interred in the Graceland Meditation Garden. Elvis stalks the world in the profound shift he made in American, and by default, world entertainment – a shift that still exists.

Elvis Presley

MARC BOLAN
(1947–1977)

GOLDERS GREEN
CREMATORIUM, LONDON,
ENGLAND
(BOLAN'S ROCK SHRINE, GIPSY
LANE, QUEENS RIDE, BARNES,
LONDON).

Marc Bolan, imbued with a lifelong fear of dying in a car accident, lost his life at age 30 when his Mini, driven by girlfriend Gloria Jones, collided with a steel reinforced fence post. His recording career, surprisingly extensive and very successful (he outsold The Who and Elton John during his lifetime), often featured lyrics laced with references to cars and shot the former child model to stardom in the Glam Rock era of the 1970s. Bolan was born Mark Feld in Stoke Newington to a Jewish lorry driver father and a Christian mother and grew up in southwest London. It was in Wimbledon that he began his lifelong fascination with rock and his obsession with stardom. His name, a contraction of Bo(b) (Dy)lan, was one in a list of identities that Mark Feld adopted – Toby Tyler and Bowland were others – and he spent much of the late sixties in

a series of failed attempts at stardom. Bolan, more than most, was exploited by the ferociously self-interested managers of pop music. His second manager Allan Warren sold his contract to David Kirsch in lieu of rent – Kirsch did nothing with the contract until Bolan's mother insisted it be torn up. He was signed to Decca in 1965, and under the control of Simon Napier Bell (the then manager of The Yardbirds) Bolan was slotted into the band John's Children, a viable live act but one of little recording worth.

After these debacles Bolan reassessed himself and found a new direction in mythical poetry and fantasy writing, producing two novels and a book of poetry (*Warlock of Love*, which sold 40,000 copies). These ideas eventuated in Tyrannosaurus Rex, a psychedelic folk-rock duo. Tyrannosaurus Rex recorded four albums and three of their singles hummed around the charts, but Bolan was playing with the formula and with the expansion of the band came the shortening of the name to T. Rex. A grittier sound and Bolan's signature Les Paul came with

Marc Bolan

the single 'Ride a White Swan' as did the glitter painted cheeks, suggested by Bolan's new wife June Child. Glam rock was born.

A succession of hits followed – 'Hot Love', 'Get it On', 'Telegram Sam', 'Metal Guru', 'Jeepster' and by 1972, Tyrannosaurus Rex were selling 100,000 records a day world-wide and accounting for 6% of British domestic record sales. Amped up by his boy-girl persona and gritty performances and sound, Marc Bolan was a star.

Bolan was in demand, recording with Electric Light Orchestra and playing guitar with Ike and Tina Turner, but his development of a more complex sound, almost a return to the Tyrannosaurus Rex sound, saw the original Tyrannosaurus Rex line-up disintegrate, as did his marriage. A growing love of brandy and cocaine made him more corpulent and his teenage fan-base looked elsewhere.

He recorded a new album in 1977, *Dandy in the Underworld* and toured with The Damned to widen his appeal, but time had moved on and as his great friend and rival David Bowie matured away from Glam to set the direction of the next decade, Marc Bolan floundered. It was at this point that his life ended. In 2013 the shrine on Gipsy Lane was listed on a BBC program as one of Britain's holiest places.

Marc Bolan

RONALD 'BON' SCOTT
(1946–1980)

FREMANTLE CEMETERY, WESTERN AUSTRALIA

Larrikin charm and rock and roll attitude through and through, Ronald Belford Scott exemplified the hard knocks and endless drive that immigrant Brits brought to the burgeoning rock scene in Australia in the sixties and seventies. Bon Scott was born on July 9, 1946 in Forfar, Angus, Scotland to 'Chick' Scott and his wife 'Isa' Mitchell. The young family, with brother Derek, emigrated on assisted passage to Melbourne and then to Fremantle in Western Australia.

Bon began learning the drums in the Fremantle Scots Pipe band, attended John Curtin College of the Arts but dropped out and spent nine months at Riverbank Juvenile Institution at age 15 (on charges of unlawful carnal knowledge, providing a false name and theft). He was considered too socially maladjusted for the military. So, his characteristic anti-authoritarianism erupted and stayed with him for the rest of his life making his way into Rock.

After mundane work, Scott started his first band The Spektors, as drummer and occasional singer. The band merged with Vince Lovegrove's band, The Valentines and they went on to become a top 30 act, but drug scandals and musical differences saw Scott joining Fraternity, a song-writing cooperative where Scott learned his craft, honing lyrics and melody. The band had variable success in the early 1970s before Scott had a raging argument with a band member on May 3, 1974, stormed out, drunk, and crashed his motorbike. Scott was comatose for three days and hospitalised for another three weeks. During his recovery, Lovegrove (now a manager and agent) gave Scott odd jobs and introduced him to AC/DC. Scott thought they were too inexperienced and unable to rock. The band thought that Scott was too old for them but a jam changed their minds and Scott joined in 1974.

'High Voltage' was released in 1975 and 'TNT' quickly followed but their international impact came from a compilation – also entitled 'High Voltage'. The popular song 'Dirty Deeds Done Dirt Cheap' was released in 1976, but only in Australia. Successes followed with 'Let There Be Rock' and 'Powerage'. The band's sixth album titled *Highway to Hell* established the band as a powerful hard rock act in the US and, consequently, around the world.

Ronald 'Bon' Scott

On February 19, 1980, a freezing night in London, Scott attended a session which was to be his last recorded work. Four nights later, after a heavy drinking session at The Music Machine in Camden Town, Scott passed out in his friend's car in East Dulwich. The following morning he was found lifeless and pronounced dead on arrival at King's College Hospital. The cause of death was acute alcoholic poisoning, exacerbated by Scott's asthma and the extreme cold. He was 33.

A member of AC/DC for only six years, Scott's legacy became enormous, as he reached iconic status in Australia and received recognition from around the world on his qualities as a front man. It is rumoured that 90 young women called AC/DC offices, on hearing of his death, claiming to be Bon's girlfriend. His gravesite has become a cultural landmark, the Metropolitan Cemeteries Board embellishing it with an arch and gate entrance to mark his accomplishments – an embodiment of the hard rock scene in Australia.

JOHNNY CASH
(1932–2003)

HENDERSONVILLE MEMORY GARDENS, HENDERSONVILLE, TENNESSEE, USA

Under the black granite slab at the Cash Carter Memorial, laying next to his wife, lies the 'Man in Black' Johnny Cash. His original gravestone simply acknowledged his signature hit and mantra, 'I Walk the Line.' Born in Kingsland, Arkansas, as J.R. Cash, Johnny Cash went on to become a country music icon and perhaps its most successful crossover artist. As singer-songwriter Cash became inspiration to waves of musicians in the country and gospel genres and gained respect and recognition from artists as diverse as Bob Dylan and Nine Inch Nails.

Cash was born into poverty and his family worked cotton fields, a profession he joined at age five. His elder brother, Jack was pulled into a saw and eviscerated while Johnny was working with him. Cash spoke of this as one the fundamental moments of his life, testing and reaffirming his faith in Christianity, the images haunting him until his death. It is unclear whether Johnny carried some responsibility or guilt for the incident. Cash was a gifted singer with a soprano

voice that later developed into bass baritone. He sang in the fields and on radio stations while at school, principally gospel music, which was his main love as a genre. He enlisted in the US Army in July 1950 and was stationed in Landsberg, Germany, where he formed his first band. On discharge in 1954 he moved to Memphis, Tennessee and married his childhood sweetheart Vivian Liberto. Cash sang with the Tennessee Two at night and after initially being rejected by Sam Phillips at Sun Records, was taken on when he began to write and record original material, rather than his favoured gospel.

'Folsom Prison Blues' and 'I Walk the Line' became enormous hits in 1957 and soon Cash was Sun Records biggest earner. The relentless and difficult country circuit, however, also introduced Cash to alcohol and amphetamines (used widely by performers), a problem that would not desert him. This contributed to his outlaw image. Although he never served a prison sentence, there were several events connected to drug use and other misdemeanours which landed him in jail seven times, each stay lasting a single night. The mid 1960s saw Cash reach the high point of his addiction, the breakdown of his first marriage and his new marriage to June Carter. Cash's time recording with Carter reinvigorated his career, and the singles 'Jackson' and 'Ring of Fire' still remain iconic country tracks. In 1970 he stopped using drugs, recorded 'Johnny Cash at San Quentin' and began *The Johnny Cash Show* on the ABC network – mixing a range of mainstream performers with country icons, earning him performances for American Presidents.

More and more Cash appeared in his trademark black, a symbol of his activism for the poor, the aged, and those 'betrayed by drugs'. His career started to wane in the late 1970s and was only reinvigorated by recording with The Highwaymen in the 80s.

His battle with addiction had resurfaced in 1977 and he spent much time in the 80s in and out of clinics. Cash and June Carter made sporadic appearances on TV programs, or sd guest features on records, but Cash struggled to make an impact. He turned to gospel, religious recordings and writing, but his health was failing, as was his wife's. June Carter died in 2003 and he followed her less than four months later from complications that arose from a bout of pneumonia.

Johnny Cash described himself as 'the biggest sinner ever' and he presented

himself to the world as a contradictory and conflicted man. Perhaps that is his appeal; a man of hardship and undeniable gifts, uncertain of this life but bound in faith for the next.

MICHAEL JACKSON
(1958–2009)

FOREST LAWN MEMORIAL PARK, HOLLYWOOD HILLS, CALIFORNIA, USA

Controversial, blindingly talented, innovative, and a global cultural icon, Michael Jackson dominated popular music in the 1980s and 90s. Publically, physically and visually, no other performer and artist defined oddity more than Jackson, and no other was worshipped more for what he could do.

Jackson was the eighth child of Joe and Katherine Jackson, both of whom had performed musically in Gary, Indiana. Joe and Katherine had recognised the talent in their children. Joe in particular determined to fashion them into a viable musical outfit that would become 'The Jackson Five'. From a young age they began to work the 'chitlin' circuit' as an opening act for RnB artists.

After relocating to LA, it became apparent that Michael was the supreme talent in the group and their 'teeny bop' success centred on his singing and dancing.

With a move to Epic Records, their music matured and Michael's career blossomed with solo releases that generated enormous income and culminating

with the biggest selling album of all time, *Thriller,* in 1982. His success crossed over racial boundaries and was cemented by the burgeoning MTV network. The elaborate dance routines and ambitious video clips ensured unprecedented success; Michael's 'moonwalk' became a cultural phenomenon, he had 13 No.1 singles and the biggest recording deals ever. Jackson continued to innovate, however, with blinding success came the emergence of his eccentricities.

By the mid 80s Jackson skin had begun to lighten – possibly due to lupus, but confirmed as vitiligo – the cause of each undetermined, but it is rumoured be related to skin lightening chemicals. Jackson undertook plastic surgery to remove obvious African American characteristics and was becoming more reclusive. 'Wacko Jacko' stories maintained his presence in the media.

In the early 90s, Jackson gave a televised interview during which he discussed his abusive childhood and his fractious relationship with his father. It was his infantile behaviour and suspension from reality that suggested Jackson's father was domineering and aggressive. Jackson believed he had missed out on much of his childhood years. His indulgence culminated in the creation of Neverland Ranch – a childish fantasy world. Neverland was the site of the first allegations of child sexual abuse made against Jackson in 1993. After a year of sordid allegations, Jackson allegedly paid $22 million to his accusers and was never prosecuted.

Jackson married twice in quick succession in the 1990s, once to Lisa Marie Presley and shortly after to Deborah Rowe, who was the mother of his children. Jackson's career was stagnating and a second round of sexual accusations in 2003 saw Jackson strip-searched by LAPD officers looking for evidence about Jackson's 'intimate' appearance. Emotionally, Jackson never recovered from the experience but was eventually acquitted. His eccentricities did not abate and indulgent spending, family 'influence' and possible misappropriation eventually saw Jackson close his beloved 'Neverland' ranch. The property had been used for years as collateral on multi-million dollar loans.

Jackson was in rehearsal for a massive world tour when he died at the rented mansion at 100 North Carolwood Drive in LA. He was under the 'care' of Conrad Murray, his personal physician at the time, who was later found culpable in the death for prescribing and administering anaesthetics to Jackson regularly.

Michael Jackson

Jackson's body was entombed at Forest Lawn Memorial Park's Hall of Liberty on September 3, 2009. News of his death on June 25 crashed search engines around the world, breaking records and making news, as his prodigious talent and quirkiness had in life.

Michael Jackson

WHITNEY HOUSTON
(1963–2012)

FAIRVIEW CEMETERY, WESTFIELD, NEW JERSEY, USA

With possibly the most pure mezzo soprano voice ever heard in popular music culture, Whitney Houston was singing royalty whose career serves as another tragic reminder of what can happen when dramatic success, wealth and drug abuse distort our view of ourselves.

Born in Newark, New Jersey, to a middle class family closely connected to singing royalty (her mother is a cousin to Dionne and Dee Dee Warwick), Whitney Houston began performing in gospel choirs at age 11. She joined her mother on stage for cameo appearances by age 14. She was also a sought-after model in her teenager years, but her mother 'Cissy', a powerful influence on her until her marriage, kept Whitney in school. Her mother insisted she graduate before she signed recording contracts. Houston eventually signed worldwide with Arista in 1983, age 19.

By 1986 she was nominated for three Grammy awards with a 'Record of the

Year' nomination for 'Greatest Love of All', but phenomenal success was to come in 1987 with the eponymous *Whitney* album and the monster hit 'I Wanna Dance with Somebody (Who Loves Me)'. Her light pop style cut across demographics and despite accusations of selling out, the album sold nine million copies in the US and 20 million worldwide. 'The Voice' had arrived. Her success was tied closely to romantic ballads and her career and sales peaked with the soundtrack performance of 'I Will Always Love You' from her film *The Bodyguard*, which was No.1 in the US for 14 weeks. She exploited this vein for the remainder of her career, with collaborations that ensured a mainstream appeal that could outrun the vagaries of popular appeal. The maintenance of her voice, however, was the essence of her success.

Soon after her marriage to rapper Booby Brown, problems began.

Houston met her husband-to-be in 1989 at the Soul Train Music Awards. A talented singer, writer and dancer, Brown was hardening his image after initial boy band success and was drawn increasingly to rap and house music. His lifestyle reflected that interest and the pair were exposed to increasing drug use. Despite the birth of a child, Bobbi in 1993, Houston's behaviour was becoming more and more reckless. Despite the 'good girl' reputation she had carefully crafted, she now became erratic in performance and unprofessional in attitude – failing to show for TV performances or appearing heavily affected when in public – often to the point of embarrassment. Her appearance changed dramatically; bloated and uncertain, her language was confused and the treasure that was her voice began to evaporate.

Houston's problems appeared to culminate in Bobby Brown's reality TV series 'Being Bobby Brown' with raw footage of the couple bursting their public reputation. The turmoil came to a head in 2007 when the couple divorced, and Houston gave interviews confirming her drug abuse and 'losing herself'. Her public performances deteriorated, however, with the British media describing her as 'shambolic' and 'weird' despite her continued (but much limited) recording projects.

Houston was becoming a parody of herself. She looked to work again in film to re-establish her fame, but to no avail. She visited rehearsals for a pre-Grammy

awards party on February 8, 2012 and sang poorly. Two days later she was dead, found drowned in her bath at the Beverly Hilton Hotel, unresponsive, the result a combination of heart disease and cocaine use. Four other drugs, including prescription medication and marijuana, were also found in her system. She was 48 years old.

An invitation only memorial was held at the New Hope Baptist Church in Newark on February 18, 2012. Kevin Costner, her 'Bodyguard' co-star spoke eloquently at the service. Houston's remains lie in Fairview Cemetery, Westfield, New Jersey.

Another prodigious talent taken by excess. Amongst the talented and the vulnerable it seems only the drugs change, but the same miserable outcome remains.

Chapter Five

INFAMOUS

JAMES DEAN
(1931–1955)

PARK CEMETERY, FAIRMOUNT, INDIANA, USA

Cultural icon of rebelliousness, teenage idol and film star, James Byron Dean lived his life to the fullest. Young and desired, he cut his way through the world of Hollywood, incandescent for a moment, before dying in a tragic car accident. In death his star was set, his stay on this earth all too brief.

James Dean was born in Indiana in 1931, but his father moved the family to Santa Monica, California to pursue his career as a dentist. Tragedy struck early in Dean's life when his mother died of cancer in 1940. His father, unable to care for him, sent Dean back to Indiana to be raised by his aunt and uncle in a Quaker household in Fairmont. His father served in World War II and remarried soon after. Lacking a strong father figure, Dean gravitated to a local Methodist minister, James DeWeerd who fashioned his interests in car racing, bullfighting and theatre. It was later alleged by Dean that DeWeerd abused him sexually. Biographers have maintained that the relationship was mutual.

A popular student, Dean moved back to live with his father and stepmother in

1949 and began pre-law study but soon transferred to UCLA, majoring in drama. This estranged him from his father and he dropped out of UCLA to pursue a full time acting career in 1951. All the elements for his portrayal of *Rebel Without a Cause* were there. Dean worked as a parking lot attendant at CBS studios where he met Rogers Brackett, an important player in the advertising world. He moved into Brackett's home and rumours intensified about his sexuality. Brackett who was openly gay, offered professional help and suggested that Dean move to New York to sharpen his acting skills under the tutelage of Lee Strasberg at the Actors Studio. He was the youngest actor taken into the school. Method acting became synonymous with Dean – his intensity, raw emotion and unscripted responses at the heart of his performances.

Dean performed on TV and in theatre until 1954, drawing interest eventually from Hollywood. Elia Kazan, searching for a 'young Brando', cast him in *East of Eden*. Kazan allowed Dean's impromptu character interpretations and his screen persona was established; intense, moody and unpredictable. Dean's performance in *Rebel without a Cause* connected with the hugely significant worldwide teenage market, with millions of post-war disaffected youth searching for meaning. *Giant* was Dean's last role and showcased his versatility and trademark intensity in a supporting role that actually overshadowed lead stars Rock Hudson and Elizabeth Taylor.

Dean's personal life was as intense as his onscreen personas. His relationship with actress Beverly Wills broke up after an infuriated Dean threatened a man who danced with Wills. His relationship with actress Pier Angeli ended similarly when she dumped him for singer Vic Damone. At the same time, his unwillingness to marry was covered up by studio PR who identified Dean as an 'eligible bachelor' who had not yet found the time to commit to a single woman. This was also the case for Rock Hudson and Tab Hunter, who were both gay. Dean's comment that he was not homosexual but 'would not live his life with one hand tied behind his back' is both enigmatic and revealing.

Bored between films, Dean developed an interest in car racing. He drove successfully in three races but Warner Bros. prevented him from driving during filming so his next race was not until September 30, 1955. His mechanic, Rolf

Wütherich, suggested Dean to drive to Salinas to break in the engine of his new Porshe 550 (Dean and his stunt co-ordinator Bill Hickman, travelling behind Dean, were both book for speeding earlier that day). At 5.15pm, a Ford driven by the unfortunately named Donald Turnupseed, stalled making a turn on Route 466 and Dean hurtled into the stationary car, breaking his neck and sustaining fatal injuries. Although a weak pulse was found, Dean was DOA at Paso Robles War memorial hospital at 6.20pm. Wütherich survived the crash, only to perish in another car accident in 1981.

Dean's funeral was attended by 600 mourners at Fairmount Friends Church, Indiana with 2400 packed outside. It had been four short years since he began his full-time acting career, riding the unconventional ways of Hollywood, his rebellion personified in the manner of his death.

James Dean

MARILYN MONROE
(1926–1962)

**WESTWOOD MEMORIAL PARK,
LOS ANGELES, LOS ANGELES,
CALIFORNIA, USA**

Norma Jean Mortenson would metamorphose into the most desired and most troubled of movie stars. Her public life controversial, her personal life lurching from disaster to disaster and her death shrouded in secrecy, Marilyn Monroe became the archetype of a maladjusted star and her demise was both predictable and expected.

The daughter of a very troubled Gladys Mortenson, (nee Monroe), Norma Jean's surname was changed immediately after her birth to that of Gladys' former husband, Baker. Psychologically and financially unable to care for her daughter, Norma Jean's mother placed her with foster parents at a young age, a pattern that would repeat itself in her life until the age of 16. She was married off at the age of 16 to Jim Dougherty, a friend of her foster family, to avoid a further stint in adoptive care. She moved into her mother-in-law's house whilst her husband served in World War II.

During this time she first came to public notice in a photo campaign showing the work of young women during war. She signed with the Blue Book modelling agency, dyed her hair blonde and with instant success her career had begun. She divorced Dougherty and signed with 20th Century Fox, which led to walk-ons but little else in her career, until she signed with Columbia Pictures and won her first speaking roles.

The first scandal she faced was the publication of nude photos used on calendars she posed for in 1949. Publicity at Columbia Pictures had her admit the photos were of her (she already had chin, nose and dental surgery) and claimed that the reason she had posed for the photographs was because she needed money for rent. She gave an interview discussing her upbringing and circumstances which brought sympathy for her plight as a struggling actress. Hugh Hefner used one of the unpublished shots of a nude Monroe in the first issue of *Playboy*, making her the first Playmate. The mode was set; Marilyn was to be a sex symbol. Her film roles reflected her overt sexuality while reviews commented on her poor acting.

She married and divorced Joe DiMaggio in 1954, the marriage failing because of Monroe's willingness to be portrayed sexually and DiMaggio's hatred of it. She began dating playwright Arthur Miller, a giant of the literary scene, and took acting classes with the Actors Studio to overcome her debilitating stage fright. Her taste in film roles moved to wounded women betrayed by life and lovers, and she gained some critical acclaim. Monroe's most successful role was with the comedy, *Some Like it Hot*, for which she won a Golden Globe for Best Actress. Monroe's health began to decline during filming, as she suffered a miscarriage and her worst traits were exaggerated by her heavy dependence on barbiturates and alcohol.

Her final film, *The Misfits*, written by her husband Miller, became a metaphor for her deterioration and her appearance in the film encapsulated the downfall of a Hollywood goddess. She divorced Miller in 1961 and placed herself in a variety of clinics but her dependence was such that she needed individualised care from her psychiatrist, the eminent Ralph Greenson. It was in this period that she began affairs with President John F. Kennedy and after their affair ended she turned to his brother, Robert Kennedy.

It was shortly after her much-publicised serenade of the President, 'Happy Birthday Mr President', parodying her habitual lateness and her sex appeal. Sad and pathetic she died of a 'probable suicide'. Found at 3.40am by Greenson, police were called at 4.30am at which time her housekeeper was washing bed sheets. The time of death is noted as 12:30am. Both Greenson and the housekeeper changed their stories to police and inconsistencies in forensic examination point to possible illegal behaviour. The first police on the scene believed her death to be murder. The official cause of death on the autopsy report is listed ask 'Acute Barbiturate Poisoning due to ingestion of overdose'.

The circumstances of Monroe's death contributed to the image of the Cinderella without the happy ending. She was found naked in bed, the pose a sad reinvention of the photo that had begun her career, and a final comment of the power of exploitation and the price of success. She was just 36.

Only 25 people were given permission to attend her funeral and she is interred in a pink marble crypt sealed in a bronze casket lined with satin. For 20 years Joe DiMaggio had flowers placed on her crypt three times a week. He never remarried.

Marilyn Monroe

MARTIN LUTHER KING, JR. (1929–1968)

EBENEZER BAPTIST CHURCH MEMORIAL SITE, ATLANTA GEORGIA, USA

The spoken word has never so eloquently expressed the anguish and dream of a man, as the words of Martin Luther King, Jr. did in his search for equality. His 'I Have a Dream' speech delivered the soul of a man and is universally recognised as one of the great speeches of the 20th century.

Martin Luther King, Jr. (born Michael) was born January 15, 1929, in Atlanta, Georgia. He was renamed in honour of Martin Luther, the Protestant leader of the Reformation by his father, a Baptist minister. Martin was an outspoken child and he and his father clashed (he received ferocious beatings in his adolescence), but they shared a passion to fight against injustice. Personal humiliation and dislocation from childhood friends due to race fuelled his anger and his depression, an affliction that beset him through life.

King was originally sceptical about Christianity, particularly the miracles, but he opted for the seminary as a vehicle for social change – a subject that interested him from his early teens. He was a precocious student, skipping grades, but as

part of the school debating team he once described a formative incident where he was ordered to stand on a bus for whites (according to the 'Jim Crow' laws of the day) as the angriest moment of his life.

After graduating from Morehouse College, King continued his studies at Crozer Theological College in Pennsylvania. He then took doctoral studies at Boston University and finally became pastor of Dexter Avenue Baptist Church in Montgomery, Alabama at the age of 25. King's interest in civil rights continued after a trip to India in 1959. Here, he established his views of non-violence as the means to fundamental change in the US however this means was still provocative. As leader of the Southern Christian Leadership Congress (SCLC) he took on the cause of Rosa Parks, charged under the Jim Crow laws, in the Montgomery Bus Boycott, which lasted for 385 days. King's house was bombed and the boycott saw racial segregation laws overturned in US District court. King was now a national figure in civil rights.

King believed that civil rights were the most important issue in the US in the 1950s. He conceived of a series of marches in Birmingham Alabama, Albany Georgia, St Augustine Florida, Selma Alabama, New York. Followed by the extraordinary March on Washington in August 1963 that drew a quarter of a million people to the Lincoln Memorial, which has become part of American iconography. It was here that he delivered his 'I Have a Dream' speech that created worldwide empathy for African-Americans. His constant agitation resulted in the Civil Rights Act of 1964 and King received the Nobel Peace prize for his actions.

Support for King's views was contentious in many quarters; notably the South and his success was compromised when he turned his attention to the Vietnam War. He began a systematic campaign against American involvement in the war, calling the government 'the greatest purveyor of violence in the world'. His unpatriotic statement cost white support in many states and legislatures, his writing and publication now branded as socialist. His 'Poor Peoples Campaign' was directed against military spending against the destitution of the cities and a march on Washington was organised in 1968.

On March 29 King went to Memphis Tennessee to support a black sanitary workers strike. He was accustomed to giving impromptu addresses from the

balcony of the Lorraine Motel in front of his room, 306. On April 4, at 6.01pm King was shot through the face. Despite emergency surgery, King was pronounced dead at 7.05pm at St Joseph's Hospital. He was 39.

A wave of riots across the US followed and President Johnson declared a day of mourning to calm the nation but would not attend his funeral for fear of violence.

King was refused a state funeral in his native Georgia because Governor Maddox considered him an 'enemy of the country'. At his parish of Ebenezer Baptist Church, 1300 dignitaries attended and at King's request no honours were mentioned, only his attempts to 'feed the hungry, clothe the naked, be right of the war, love and serve'

The private funeral had King's casket pulled by two mules to Morehouse College and then to South View Cemetery. His remains were exhumed in 1977 and taken to a memorial plaza near Ebenezer and laid in a marble crypt surrounded by a reflection pool.

James Earl Ray, a violent criminal, was convicted of the assassination. He was arrested in London, en route to Rhodesia, a white controlled nation in Africa.

Martin Luther King, Jr.

SHARON TATE
(1943–1969)

HOLY CROSS CEMETERY, LOS ANGELES, CALIFORNIA, USA

The peaceful and simple beauty of the Tate family grave in Holy Cross Cemetery in Los Angeles belies the horror of one of the defining moments of the 1960s. The murder of actress Sharon Tate and five others on August 9, 1969 by a group of deranged, drug-filled 'hippies' was described by the poet Joan Didion as the day 1960s 'abruptly ended' and 'the paranoia was fulfilled'.

Sharon Marie Tate was born on January 24, 1943, to career army officer Paul Tate and his wife Doris. The family moved often and by age 16 Sharon had lived in six different cities. In 1960, Paul was transferred to Italy. There Sharon became an extra in Paul Newman's *Adventures of a Young Man*, which was filming nearby, as she did with the film *Barabbas* when it was being filmed near Verona. Actor Jack Palance, impressed by her appearance and attitude, organised a screen test on her return to California. She signed a seven-year contract for Filmways, Inc. and spent the next two years learning her craft on TV's *The Beverley Hillbillies* until her first major film role came in 1965 with *Eye of the Devil*. Filmed in London, it

was there she met Polish director Roman Polanski.

Tate and Polanski admitted to having been unimpressed by each other on first meeting, but Polanski's boss, Martin Ransohoff, insisted that Tate be cast as the lead in his next project, *The Fearless Vampire Killers,* and the pair soon began a relationship. Back in Hollywood, Polanski began work on *Rosemary's Baby* while Tate was busy filming *Don't Make Waves* and *Valley of the Dolls.* Her films were mercilessly treated by critics and public alike, and Tate exuded a chilling beauty but a disposability that was disturbing. The choice of her roles, and Polanski's projects, hinted at a fascination with subjects that distorted minds would later find compelling.

They married in 1968 in London and were described as 'cool, nomadic...nicely shocking'. Polanski wanted an open, 'hippie' marriage – not conventionality. On returning to Los Angeles the couple fell into a social set of younger and older stars of the day but it was the establishment of other associations and a freedom in the house that disturbed her fellow actors. Leslie Caron later commented that the Polanskis were trusting 'to the point of recklessness' and that their house was often full of strangers.

In 1969, Tate fell pregnant and the Polanskis sought a bigger home. They found 10050 Cielo Drive, which Tate referred to as the 'love house', and was previously owned by record producer Terry Melcher and girlfriend actress Candice Bergen. Polanski was working in London, and with Tate in the last month of her pregnancy, he asked friends to stay with her until he returned on August 12.

On the night of August 8–9, Tate entertained friends Jay Sebring, Wojciech Frykowski and Abigail Folger at her home. The next morning the housekeeper Winifred Chapman discovered their bodies. Tate and Sebring were in the house, connected by a long rope looped around their necks, Fyrkowski and Folger on the front lawn. The body of a young man, later identified as Steven Parent, was found shot in his car in the driveway. Other than Parent, each of the victims had been stabbed multiple times. The word 'Pig' had been painted on the front doors in Tate's blood.

Police initially suspected William Garretson, the caretaker who was unharmed in a lodging at the back of the property, but he was released and exonerated.

Sharon Tate

Parent was a friend who had visited him that night, but Garretson did not hear anything untoward that night. When no suspects could be found the press turned on Polanski and his alleged 'open' lifestyle. Was the murder scene a satanic sacrifice careless tongues asked? Hollywood was in shock, with the rich and famous quickly abandoning town.

In November 1969 Susan Atkins, in prison for car theft, boasted she had killed Sharon Tate as well as another couple on August 9–10, Rosemary and Leno LaBianca. She incriminated charismatic drifter Charles Manson and the 'Family' – 'Tex' Watson, Patricia Krenwinkel, and Linda Kasabian – as her accomplices in the Tate murders (Lesley Van Houten and 'Clem' Grogan also took part in the LaBianca murders). Accounts from the accused described the debauched motives of the killers and the sickening actions perpetrated that night. Manson felt betrayed by Terry Melcher and the music industry. He hatched a bizarre plan

Sharon Tate

to incite a race war by slaughtering the wealthy and blaming the radical Black Panthers. Manson believed he would then be asked, messiah-like, to lead forces against the Panthers. He was aware that Melcher had moved from the house but instructed his followers to go and slaughter everyone there while he remained at the campsite at Spahn's Movie Ranch.

Kasabian and Atkins revealed terrifying details that confirmed their claims, Atkins claiming that Tate was nothing more than a store mannequin to her. Tate's voice was 'like an IBM machine talking', she said, so Atkins stabbed her to death and wrote 'Pig' on the door in Tate's blood. Atkins said Tate had begged for the life of her unborn child but she told the dying actress there would be no mercy.

The demeanour of the 'Manson Family' in court, amused and irreverent, horrified the world. The love generation had mutated into these monsters. Californian law commuted the death sentences handed down for the Tate murders on October 21, 1971 to life sentences where they remain, with the exception Atkins who died in 2009. Sharon Tate was buried with her unborn son in her arms in the family grave in Culver City. She was later joined by her mother Doris (1992) and sister Patricia (2000) who kept the Manson family behind bars with their heartfelt parole testimonies in the decades following Sharon's death.

JOHN EDGAR HOOVER
(1895–1972)

CONGRESSIONAL CEMETERY, WASHINGTON D.C., USA

A sombre and plain stone headstone in the Congressional Cemetery in Washington, D.C. belies the power of the man that rests there. J.Edgar Hoover defied Presidents, haunted his nation's capital and driven by his own sense of righteousness, stood over the public life of a nation and the private lives of its most powerful people.

John Edgar Hoover was born on New Year's Day, 1895 in Washington, D.C. of Swiss German descent to Dickerson Hoover and Anna Marie Scheitlin. Various sources, namely author Gore Vidal, believed Hoover had some African American ancestry. Hoover grew up in the Capitol Hill neighbourhood and was admired at school for his 'cool relentless logic' in debating and his singing voice. He spoke rapidly to overcome a stutter, a habit he maintained. He obtained his law degree at George Washington University Law School in 1916. A creature of Washington, he lived there his whole life.

He learnt the value of information whilst working at the Congressional Library. Employed at the Department of Justice in the War Emergency Division, he quickly

became head of the Alien Enemy Division. This appointment hardened Hoover's ultra conservative attitudes and his penchant for accumulating and filing information on individuals. By 1924 he had risen to become head of the Bureau of Investigation – the precursor to the FBI – appointed by President Coolidge, the first of six Presidents he was to 'serve'.

Faced by outlaw gangsters in the Mid-West, Hoover began a long campaign to eradicate these criminals with his G-Men ('Government Men', agents of the Federal Bureau). Although rarely in the field himself, he co-opted local Department heads to hunt down the gangs and Depression era criminals like Pretty Boy Floyd and John Dillinger. These successes elevated Hoover's profile but the vast bootlegging in the cities was not addressed and despite growing violence, Hoover denied the existence of organised crime for three decades (it was later suggested his inveterate gambling and tips from mobsters such as Frank Costello that swayed his view). His success was rewarded with the creation of the FBI in 1935; a facility to chase felons across state lines and have them charged with federal offences. The FBI effectively ended the era of the Depression gangsters.

The FBI, under the direction of Hoover, began to gather fingerprint files and establish forensic crime laboratories creating the most effective analysis of crimes in the world. Hoover also used his powers to work against subversives in World War II and it was this initiative that resulted in Hoover accumulating information on the powerful throughout society – politicians, celebrities, the wealthy and political activists. He used this information to bolster his profile. He also hid information, including the post-war counterintelligence codes used by the Soviets which he locked in his safe, choosing not to inform President Truman or the CIA.

By the mid 1950s, the FBI was being distorted by Hoover to his own mysterious ends. It was his failure to address the Mafia influence which finally began to discredit Hoover after newspapers ran stories on the Apalachin Meeting (a meeting between mob bosses to divide the country up for its spoils) in 1957. Truman and Kennedy both considered dismissing Hoover, but the existence of his hidden files of potentially damaging information spooked both Presidents.

Hoover often used innuendo to consolidate his position – he circulated rumours

John Edgar Hoover

of sexual escapades and 'deviant' sexuality against his enemies while, ironically, leading a closeted homosexual existence. His Associate Director, Clyde Tolson inherited Hoover's estate; they holidayed together for decades and shared interests in horseracing. It appears Hoover used the flaws in others to fireproof himself against claims of his homosexuality.

His grip on his world of Washington D.C. slipped when the FBI bungled and distorted investigations into Kennedy's assassination and a counterculture that challenged so many of his beliefs emerged. By the mid 1970s his influence was waning, however he maintained strong support in Congress until his death at his Washington, D.C., home on May 2, 1972, from heart disease.Hoover created a monolith and hid behind it. His control, real or rumoured, cast a pall over the intricate relationships of the powerful and in some ways undid the achievements of the past.

John Edgar Hoover

HOWARD HUGHES
(1905–1976)

GLENWOOD CEMETERY,
HOUSTON, TEXAS, USA

The model of the eccentric recluse, Howard Hughes' immense fortune and bizarre behaviour disguised a truly innovative engineer, aviator, filmmaker and investor whose vision of the world and its possibilities reshaped the fields of his endeavour. Born to a very successful family on December 24, 1905, his father Howard Hughes Snr. was an engineer and established the Hughes family fortune through the Hughes Tool Company. He invented a tool that drilled for oil but he leased the invention rather than selling it off. Hughes' uncle was the famed novelist and screenwriter Rupert Hughes.

Howard Jr.'s strength was in technology, he built Houston's first radio transmitter when he was 11 and took his first flying lesson at age 14. His mother died in 1922 and his father in 1924, and their early deaths inspired his philanthropy in medical research. He took control of 75 per cent of the vast fortune at the age of 19. He married a year later and moved to LA to make his mark as a filmmaker. His success was extraordinary and rapid. His films were nominated for Academy

awards and his World War I epic, *Hell's Angels*, was a box office smash, as was *The Outlaw*. Hughes took control of the troubled RKO Pictures and walked away after 25 years with a personal profit of $6.5 million in 1954.

Hughes' behaviour was already showing signs of OCD; he was pedantic about detail but wide-ranging in thought and action. His success in motion pictures was replicated in real estate and in avionics, his first passion. He was obsessed with creating larger and larger planes to offset the reliance on shipping in wartime. His designs were radical but his passion would become his downfall as two near fatal crashes and horrifying injuries began a spiralling dependence on codeine for pain management. Despite this, Hughes manoeuvred around financial controls to create the revolutionary Constellation. His aerospace company effectively monopolised commercial airliner design, further adding to his enormous wealth (estimated at one point as being 1/2000th of the GNP of the US).

The rejection of his massive Hercules 'Spruce Goose' by the military led to the first of Hughes' breakdowns. He spent four months in a film studio near his home – naked, watching films, eating nothing but chocolate, chicken and milk. He would write detailed notes to aides about not making eye contact and would constantly rearrange the boxes of Kleenex that surrounded him. This pattern became his existence, a reaction to his substantial injuries and his allodynia – an extreme pain reaction to touch and sensation.

Hughes' reclusiveness became the stuff of legend. He occupied hotels, largely in Vegas, Florida and the Caribbean. Beginning with the Desert Sands in Las Vegas in 1967, he would buy the hotels, occupy a whole floor and live in isolation, contacting the world through his 'Mormon Mafia'. His wife, former actress Jean Peters filed for divorce and accepted alimony of only $70,000 per annum. As Hughes' health waned, control over his vast fortune brought out those willing to manipulate him. The CIA approached him to fund the recovery of a sunken Soviet submarine, which he agreed to do; they were well aware of his obsession with the submarine film *Ice Station Zebra*, and his xenophobia of the Soviets.

Hughes died in transit to Houston Methodist Hospital on April 5, 1976. He was unrecognisable and the FBI had to use fingerprint technology to establish his identity. A subsequent autopsy noted kidney failure as the cause of death. After

years of legal dispute, his estate was distributed between 22 cousins. Terri Moore, his third and secret wife received an undisclosed settlement in 1984.

The Howard Hughes Medical Institute wholly owned his aircraft and real estate business and so he established one of the most substantial grants to medicine ever. The businesses were sold for $5.2 billion. To offset the agony of the loss of his parents as a young man, his incredible successes and extraordinary life became, in the American tradition, philanthropic. Not simply defined by eccentricity but by generosity. He lies with them at Glenwood Cemetery, Houston, Texas.

Howard Hughes

JOHN LENNON
(1940–1980)

STRAWBERRY FIELDS MEMORIAL PARK, CENTRAL PARK, NEW YORK, USA

The quintessential rebel artist, John Lennon shifted the ground in musical culture, elevating the pop song from stereotyped entertainment to observational artistic endeavour. His ground-breaking success as part of the most successful commercial band in popular music launched him into the world of politics and protest – a stance that saw him loved, vilified and sadly, murdered.

John Winston Lennon was born on October 9, 1940 in wartime London to Julia and Alfred Lennon. Named after his grandfather and Winston Churchill, his early life was disrupted by war and by a fractured family. By age five, John had been handed over to his aunt and uncle for care. He kept intermittent contact with his mother, whose rebelliousness and unconventionality he mimicked later in life. She taught him to play the banjo, encouraged his musical and artistic interests while his Aunt Mimi and Uncle George, more staid, tried to create a path for John in society. He credited his mother's behaviour with much of the pain in his writing

and acknowledged her effect on his later views on feminism. She was hit by a car and killed, walking home from visiting him. He was 17.

While at Quarry Bank High School, John formed his first band the Quarrymen. At their second performance Lennon met Paul McCartney, asked him to join and the pair began their writing collaboration at each other's homes. Both sets of parents warned Paul about John, his rebelliousness and the trouble he was destined for. The band evolved into The Beatles by 1960; playing residencies in Hamburg from 1960 to 1962 sharpened their song writing and performance skills as well as developing their taste for amphetamines.

Their image changed under the influence of manager Brian Epstein, the band broke into mainstream performance and with their debut album *Please, Please Me*, in 1962. The first stage of Beatlemania had begun. In 1964, the group made their first US appearance on *The Ed Sullivan Show*, marking their breakthrough to international stardom. Lennon found fame exhilarating at first but then confining and his acerbic wit surfaced, often deriding interviewers or outraging his audience by his audacity, (his comments on Christianity and Jesus almost ended the Beatles career in the US). This was exacerbated by his growing use of alcohol (his 'fat Elvis' phase as he named it). A reduced touring schedule allowed the song writing and production skills to shift. The ground-breaking *Sgt. Pepper* album, followed by the *White Album*, saw Lennon's lyrics deepen and the Beatles became a studio phenomenon, redefining pop music and the direction of pop culture.

The constrictions of The Beatles' existence saw rising tensions in the band. The lack of touring and John's obsessive-possessive relationship with his wife Yoko Ono were big contributors to these tensions. As well as the death of Brian Epstein, McCartney's growing hold over business and the establishment of Apple Records saw the band implode, with McCartney leaving the group and releasing a solo album riding on the controversy. A new phase in Lennon's life had begun.

Through 1970 to 1972 Lennon had worldwide success with his Plastic Ono Band. His songs were more forthright and political and his song 'Imagine' became an anti-war and humanist anthem. His move to New York and criticism of the Nixon administration saw him targeted for FBI investigations and consequently he was denied permanent residency until 1976. Lennon's artistic product started to wane;

John Lennon

his *Some Time in New York City* was criticised as indulgent and driven by issues rather than emotion – and his collaboration with Ono was vilified, as was she.

Lennon became estranged from Ono for two years (1973–1975) a time he described as his 'lost weekend' and his behaviour was becoming more alcohol fuelled and erratic. He completed his *Mind Games* album and contributed to David Bowie and Elton John's work on occasion. With his reconnection with Ono and the birth of his son, Sean, Lennon withdrew from the music industry to become a highly publicised househusband. His reconciliation with McCartney was low-key.

He re-emerged in 1980 with his album *Double Fantasy* after a five-year hiatus

On the night of December 8, 1980, Mark Chapman shot John Lennon outside of his New York apartment in the Dakota. It had only been four hours earlier that evening, that Lennon had autographed a copy of *Double Fantasy* for Chapman. He was pronounced dead at 11:07pm at Roosevelt Hospital. Ono declared there would be no funeral, and she had his body cremated and his ashes scattered in Central Park where the Strawberry Fields Memorial now stands.

Lennon was 40 years old, a legend in his own lifetime, a brilliant career cut far too short.

John Lennon

JOHN BELUSHI
(1949–1982)

ABEL'S HILL CEMETERY, CHILMARK, MARTHA'S VINEYARD, MASSACHUSETTS, USA

'Gross-out' comedy has become a Hollywood staple as a genre … highly successful and increasingly influential in popular culture. This style of comedy evolved from the influence of John Belushi and his performances on *Saturday Night Live,* another American staple. But it is not just his comedic influence that Belushi is remembered for – his death has also become a Hollywood staple. The circumstances of his death are embroiled in controversy and mystery, either disguising the man, or revealing the subculture that only insiders in the movie machine know and understand.

John Belushi was born of Albanian parentage in Humboldt Park on the west side of Chicago Illinois. Raised in the Albanian Orthodox Church his early life was conventional and unremarkable. He attended Wheaton Warrenville High School, as did his future wife, Judy Jacklin.

A keen interest in comedy, particularly physical comedy, led him to form his own comedy troupe in 1971. The group held a residency at Second City Comedy where he met Harold Ramis and Dan Aykroyd, of Ghostbusters fame. In 1973 Belushi and Jacklin moved to New York to work for National Lampoon Radio as writer, director, and actor, and then as an original cast member of *Saturday Night Live*. He and Jacklin married in 1976. This conventional progression in career disguised a heavy reliance on drugs and alcohol, a lifestyle freely admitted by his wife who shared his habits which continued despite observations from guests on the show with Belushi.

Belushi became a more prominent and dominant influence on *SNL* after Chevy Chase left for Hollywood. It was this increase in popularity that lead to his role in *Animal House,* his breakout film, which cost less than three million dollars to make the film but grossed $141 million. Belushi's growing interest in music was funnelled into *The Blues Brothers* with Aykroyd, which originally featured on *SNL.* The resulting film in 1980 has since become a cult classic and Belushi appeared to have made it to Hollywood, but the failure of several film projects saw his mainstream, romantic lead

John Belushi

appeal falter. There was another reality to Belushi; his gross out screen persona was a reflection of his heavy cocaine use, violent temper and kamikaze approach to life. Despite desperate attempts to straighten up including the employment of trainers (primarily as drug minders), Belushi was spiralling out of control.

His death confirmed the rumours. On March 5, 1982, his trainer Bill Wallace found Belushi dead in Bungalow 3 at Chateau Marmont on Sunset Boulevard. The cause of death was a 'speedball' – a combination of cocaine and heroin – which had been administered by Cathy Smith. Two months later, Smith admitted in an interview with the *National Enquirer* that she had given him the fatal drugs. She had been allowed to leave the scene by LAPD despite having a syringe and spoon in her effects. Found guilty of involuntary manslaughter, Smith later served 15 months in prison. The reality was that Belushi was creating a fantasy for people – and it was the reality of actually living that fantasy that contributed to his death. His gravestone was emblazoned with '...Rock and roll lives on.' An icon for excess, his headstone had been vandalised so often that his remains were removed to a secret location in Abel Hill Cemetery, Martha's Vineyard, Massachusetts, to give him rest.

KAREN CARPENTER
(1950–1983)

Pierce Brothers Valley Oaks Memorial Park, Los Angeles, California, USA

The saccharin melodies and pop friendly arrangements disguised the sad internal existence of the very successful 70s music duo of The Carpenters and the media focus for the group, Karen Carpenter. Talented musician and hyper successful, Karen fell to a new type of demon, rather the industry standards of cocaine and heroin. Her death, and the secrecy of her travails in life, revealed for many young women a world that had been secret.

Karen Carpenter was born on March 2, 1950 in New Haven, Connecticut. Her family relocated to Los Angeles in 1963 and it was at this time she was influenced by her brother's prodigious talent as a pianist. She joined the school band at Downey High School but was disappointed with her assignment of the glockenspiel and asked to play the drums. Her talent was obvious and she and her brother made recordings in 1965 and went on to form the Richard Carpenter Trio. They also performed with an ensemble named Spectrum – both groups focusing on

harmonies and mainstream pop sounds. Many rejections from record companies followed but eventually, by 1969 A&M Records signed The Carpenters. Karen had already been dieting since 1967.

Karen was the lead vocalist on *the Offering* and Richard Carpenter wrote most of the songs but it was the next album, *Close to You* in 1970 that cemented their success with massive hits 'We've Only Just Begun' and 'Close to You'. With this success Karen was forced out from behind her drum kit and into the spotlight and touring pressures mounted. Richard Carpenter developed a dependency on Quaaludes, forcing frequent concert cancellations and ending touring completely in September 1978. The band relied heavily on TV appearances to maintain their profile. Their final album *Made in America* was released in 1981. Richard Carpenter could no longer perform and took a year off to deal with his addiction. During this time Karen made a solo album, experimenting with new sounds and vocals. Unfortunately, the record company decided it would not be released and claimed $400,000 in recording costs from Karen. She was devastated.

Karen lived with her parents until age 26. She and her brother bought real estate together to consolidate their wealth. Karen dated several well-known Hollywood identities until she met and married real estate developer, Thomas Burris, in a whirlwind romance. He was nine years her senior and had deceived her about his wish for children (his previous wife had insisted on a vasectomy). Their marriage only lasted 14 months.

By 1982 Karen's physical condition was becoming apparent; her secret had started to emerge. She had been receiving treatment from a psychotherapist for anorexia. She had been secretly taking thyroid medication to speed up her metabolism and laxatives to control her weight. Despite therapy her conditioned worsened and was admitted to hospital in New York. She gained 15 kilograms in eight weeks but constant physical strain induced by self-medication had weakened her heart and she was found dead at her parent's home a month before her 33rd birthday. Traces of a powerful emetic were found in her body, her quest for 'perfection', driven by the pressures to perform, had emaciated her body on all levels.

She was originally entombed at Forest Lawn Memorial Park but in 2003 her

Karen Carpenter

brother had her reinterred with her parents in the family mausoleum at Pierce Brothers Valley Oaks Memorial Park in Westlake, California.

Karen Carpenter's fragility, her delusions about perfection and the consequences of trying to maintain that standard, are a cautionary tale for those we admire and those who hide within themselves.

Karen Carpenter

PRINCESS DIANA
(1961–1997)

SPENCER ESTATE GROUNDS, ALTHORP, LONDON, ENGLAND

Swooningly beautiful, betrayed by her husband, tragically killed, universally mourned and admired – Diana, Princess of Wales, is the modern-day Princess. The life and death of Princess Diana epitomises that of the gorgeous outsider who shook the stodgiest of British institutions to its foundations.

Of aristocratic birth, the Spencers had been associates of the British Royal Family for generations. Diana's parents divorced when she was eight and she was educated at a variety of schools but showed little academic ability other than excelling in music, she was an accomplished pianist. She was first associated with Prince Charles when he was linked to her elder sister but his interest piqued when she was a guest at a country weekend. The Palace had pressured Prince Charles for some time to find a suitable wife. The coquettish Diana teased the world press, and the match royal watchers had hoped for was announced in February 1981.

The wedding of the century followed on July 29, 1981, viewed by 750 million

people worldwide. Diana stunned the world – a phenomenon had arrived – and the Palace was astounded by the popularity of the Princess of Wales. Her first pregnancy followed quickly, and Prince William was born in June 1982. Prince Harry followed in September 1984, the succession assured but not the marriage.

The Royal couple toured extensively and the constant attention on Diana began to form a rift with Charles. His carefully stage managed veneer of the king in waiting, was being upstaged by his beautiful wife and her attitude towards schooling and care of her children. Strains on the marriage began to appear, which were exacerbated by Charles' continuation of an affair with his now wife, Camilla Parker-Bowles. The breakdown of the marriage was at first denied, but then strategically placed publications and interviews manufactured by Diana sidestep their closed circle and damaged the Monarchy. She admitted her adultery, but only after the breakdown of her marriage.

Charles countered this with his comment of 'irretrievable breakdown' of his marriage instigated by Diana, fuelled by her inability to cope with the enormous pressure of the 'job'. The world listened and watched in awe at the highly personalised confessions which provided a rare insight into an institution largely hidden from public view. As a result, the Queen wrote to Diana and Charles to ask for an early divorce. Typically Charles' announcement of terms was countered with Diana's own agreement after negotiations, and the battle for the hearts of the public would continue.

Diana's life after the divorce was just as fascinating for the press. Her relationships with Hasnat Khan and Dodi Fayed were scrutinised and commentary about possible 'deaths threats' from her former husband fuelled the press' obsession with her. This was no more brutally demonstrated than by the manner of her death.

Diana, Dodi Fayed and driver Henri Paul were fatally injured in a car crash in Paris in the Pont de l'Alma tunnel on the night of August 31 1997. Eventually, the accident was attributed to grossly negligent driving and harassment by the paparazzi. Conspiracy theories abound, largely fuelled by a decade long campaign by Mohamed Al Fayed, Dodi's father. The accusations included MI6 and the Duke of Edinburgh as co-conspirators, but these wild claims were tabled and quickly

dismissed in subsequent enquiries.

Following the fatal accident, Charles escorted Diana's body from France to London. Her funeral was held in Westminster Abbey on September 6, 1997 and broadcast live to the entire world. That day will be remembered for the extraordinary outpouring expressed in flowers at the palace and the curt speech delivered by her brother explaining that she needed no royal title '...to generate... magic', a reference to the callous withdrawal of titles insisted upon by the palace. She lies at Althorp House, the ancestral home of the Spenser's.

Perhaps Diana's greatest appeal came not from her beauty or her tragedy but from her position and her ability to show us intimacies of a world that had been hidden by pretence and power. She defined herself as a woman rather than being shaped, shackled and controlled by those around her. Much of Diana's life was defined by pictures; her dress backlit as she was first introduced to the media, sitting forlornly alone at the Taj Mahal in 1991, swinging in the arms of actor John Travolta on a US visit and her kiss with Charles on the balcony at Buckingham Palace.

Diana paid with her life, at the hands of those who would possess her, the public. In that sense, she was really the peoples' princess.

Princess Diana

Chapter Six

FILM AND TV

HUMPHREY BOGART
(1899–1957)

FOREST LAWN MEMORIAL PARK, LOS ANGELES, CALIFORNIA, USA

The antithesis of his screen image, a man who could never take himself seriously, Humphrey Bogart's acting craft was to him, the ultimate and earned him the accolade of being rated the greatest film star in 20th Century American cinema. Humphrey DeForest Bogart was born on December 25, 1899 in New York City the only son of a wealthy surgeon and a highly successful art director, Bogart had a privileged but emotionally bereft childhood, once describing a kiss as 'an event' in his family. As a child he spent time creating theatre with his sisters at the 55-acre estate in upstate New York.

Bogart attended prestigious schools but was ultimately expelled from the elite Phillips Academy. He joined the US navy towards the end of World War I, indulging his love of the sea. At the same time, in uncertain circumstances, he damaged his upper lip – said to be the result of a war-time accident or the result of a bar room brawl – which accentuated his slight lisp.

On discharge, he worked variously as a shipper and bond salesman. His career options were a great disappointment to his family, he settled on a career in acting and stated, 'I was born to be indolent and this was the softest of rackets'. He was a persistent and steady performer and found roles in 17 Broadway productions between 1922 and 1935. Along the way, he perfected his distinctive voice and threatening mannerisms, as well as a damaging alcohol problem and a penchant for marrying older women – Bogart married four times. With the onset of the Depression, Bogart headed to Hollywood and made his first films with Fox Film in 1930 and 1931. He shuffled between Hollywood and New York and in 1934 his father died, swamped in debt from bad investments, which Bogart eventually paid off. On his return to Hollywood he made his breakthrough film *The Petrified Forest* in 1936, which was based on his stage lay of the same name and was a huge box office success. Despite its success he remained a B-movie lead and character actor, making an average of six movies a year.

Bogart's friendships with important directors and writers eventually led him to roles that would establish his star status and he made a series of films that would become classics. Starting with *High Sierra* (1941), *The Maltese Falcon* (1941), *Casablanca* (1942), and with Lauren Bacall, *To Have and Have Not* (1944) and *The Big Sleep* (1945). These films cemented his anti-hero persona and established his reputation as a romantic lead.Bogart's love life became the focus of much press speculation after his appearances with Bacall. She was 19, he was 44 and after three failed marriages (all to actresses who were heavy drinkers with explosive personalities, which was very much in the mould of his mother) the sexual chemistry on screen fuelled their personal relationship. Bogart and Bacall married on May 21, 1945.

In 1948 Bogart began his own production company, Santana Productions, to exploit his new power in the industry. Perhaps his best performance was in *The Treasure of the Sierra Madre* (1948) where his on-screen character morphs from a likeable 'Joe' to paranoid psychopath after a group of gold prospectors strike it rich.

Working outside of his own production company he made *The African Queen* in 1951, taking profits rather than salary. The film, shot in the Congo, was an

enormous success. He followed with *The Caine Mutiny* in 1954, but years of alcohol abuse and chain smoking were taking their toll. His final screen appearance was in 1956's *The Harder They Fall*. Bogart contracted oesophageal cancer but he put off his diagnosis until it was obvious he was seriously ill. Despite surgery and chemotherapy he succumbed on January 14, 1957.

The elite of Hollywood attended his funeral, and John Huston delivered his eulogy, he commented that Bogie's caustic observations kept all of the pretentious on guard. At heart, Bogart was an old-fashioned gentleman. His friend, director John Huston, observed that in the characters he played, perhaps Bogart found a sense of himself ... lost and alone, a melancholy anti-hero rather than the abrasive fast-talking gangster.

'Bogie' was buried at Forest Lawn Memorial Park Cemetery with a gold whistle inscribed with the famous line Bacall delivered to him in their debut film, *To Have and Have Not*: 'If you want anything, just whistle.'

Humphrey Bogart

ERROL FLYNN
(1909–1959)

FOREST LAWN MEMORIAL PARK, LOS ANGELES, CALIFORNIA, USA

Possibly no other man of the modern era had his life encapsulated by sexual athleticism as much as Errol Leslie Thomson Flynn. Generations are familiar with the expression 'in like Flynn' and such a raucous and unbridled sense of sexual prowess and libertine existence was rarely captured on the public stage. Just as Don Juan and Casanova were referenced in their context, so was Errol Flynn.

Despite Australian-born Flynn describing his family as seafaring people, he was actually the son of a Professor of Biology and received a highly privileged education in Hobart, London and Sydney. He was dismissed from Church of England Grammar (Shore school, Sydney) for petty theft (probably to procure alcohol), and, according to Flynn an early sexual assignation with the school's laundress.

He sought adventure in New Guinea but returned to Sydney to try his hand at acting in 1933, landing a leading role *In the Wake of the Bounty*. This propelled him

to London, and after a stint acting there on the stage he was offered a leading role in *Murder at Monte Carlo* and was signed to Warner Bros. as a contract actor. His lead in *Captain Blood* (1935) made him an overnight sensation under the direction of Michael Curtiz. This was the first of several swashbuckling films that cemented his fame. By 1940 he was the fourth most popular actor in the US and demanding $200,000 a film.

The end of World War II saw dramatic changes in taste of the American movie-going audience and by 1950 Flynn had been removed from the roster of stars. This may also have been exacerbated by his reputation; he was often linked romantically with his co-stars and married three times. Flynn also had many health issues; he had recurrent malaria, which he had contracted in New Guinea, he had already had one heart attack by 1942, chronic back pain medicated by morphine and heroin, lingering tuberculosis, a penchant for cocaine and various venereal diseases. As a naturalised American, he was drafted but failed the fitness test, which became a damaging image problem for him. He was charged in 1942, a pivotal year for Flynn, with the statutory rape of two 15-year-old girls. He escaped on the back of character assassination of the girls by his lawyer, but the reporting of the case in the world press effectively ended Flynn's career in Hollywood.

He spent the remainder of his life drifting from one financial failure to another – poorly made films, self-promotional exercises and ventures in the Caribbean and the Mediterranean. His body bloated, he became a parody of his swashbuckling screen image, haunting ports and drinking with a dwindling list of friends and half-baked business associates. He made a comeback of sorts as a character actor in the late 1950s in such films as *The Sun Also Rises* (1957) and *Too Much Too Soon* (1958), but his health was deteriorating.

Flynn was negotiating a lease for his yacht with Vancouver businessman, George Caldough, when he died. He was being driven to the airport for an LA flight when he complained of worsening back and leg pain. Caldough took him to a doctor friend, Grant Gould, who administered a painkiller and allowed Flynn to rest after leg manipulation. He returned 20 minutes later to find Flynn unconscious and unresponsive. The 50-year-old actor was pronounced dead at Vancouver General

Errol Flynn

Hospital at 7:45pm, October 14, 1959.

The coroner commented on his appearance describing him as a tired old man, old before his time.

Errol Flynn wanted to be buried in his beloved Bahamas. Flynn's grave, an elegant and understated headstone, belies a man who shook the world of entertainment, a stellar opportunist and one who used the world for a fleeting time, to make his own.

Errol Flynn

WALT DISNEY
(1901–1966)

FOREST LAWN MEMORIAL PARK, LOS ANGELES, CALIFORNIA, USA

The delight in fantasy worlds, charming and innocent, untroubled and ideal, came through the eyes of a man who identified the heart and soul of America. Simple and uncomplicated on screen, innovative and imaginative in reimaging built environments, the creativity of Walt Disney has coloured our world from the 1920s to the present day.

Walter Elias Disney was born on December 5, 1901 to Elias and Flora Disney in Hermosa Chicago, Illinois. Much of Walt's early life was on the move as his father sought and pursued business opportunities from Canada to Florida to Missouri to Kansas, where the family settled long enough for Walt to attend school for a substantial period. His grades were poor but his interest in drawing developed at Kansas City Art Institute in Saturday classes. This continued after a move back to Chicago until Walt dropped out of school and enlisted, only to be rejected on age (he was 16). He volunteered to become an ambulance driver for the Red Cross in France for a year and on his return he headed back to Kansas City.

It was in Kansas City that Walt discovered the E.G. Lutz book on animation and began a small business creating animated fairy tales called 'Laugh-o-grams'. Locally successful but unable to sustain him, he moved the business to Hollywood with money he pooled from his brother and his accounts. Disney Studious opened in 1923. Here he met his wife, Lillian, an ink and paint illustrator and they were married in 1925.

Disney's successes came slowly, the creation of characters to feature in short animations was a difficult task. Early character's like Alice (real life actress surrounded by animation) and Oswald the Rabbit were hits but their success waned quickly. Real success didn't come until Walt created Mickey Mouse (a variety of previous incarnations existed) and featured him with a soundtrack voicing the character. Mickey's popularity grew throughout the 1930s and was consolidated by the use of Technicolor 3-Strip with shorts like *The Three Little Pigs* (most successful short of all time). Disney had learnt that an emotionally gripping story line was vital to success in animations and created a separate story department at the studio, another innovation that catapulted Disney to leadership in the field. Spin off characters became just a successful – Donald Duck, Goofy and Pluto. Disney was planning another challenging innovation; a full length animated feature using realistic human animation. After a gestation of four years and more problems with finance (a Disney trait), *Snow White and the Seven Dwarfs* was released and earned the equivalent of ($US today) $134 million dollars in ticket sales.

The film allowed for larger Disney studios to be built in Burbank and other very successful features followed; *Pinocchio*, *Fantasia*, *Bambi* and *Alice in Wonderland*. These productions allowed Disney to experiment with live action documentary style nature films that would become a mainstay of the burgeoning TV market and the design and building of his enduring legacy, Disneyland. Disney had been toying with the idea of a theme park since visiting Argentina and seeing a child's theme park in La Plata. His idea came to fruition in 1955 where the various 'lands' of Disney Land was opened, surrounded by a miniature locomotive (an obsession with Disney since his childhood) – a place where 'dreams come true'.

The extraordinary success of Disneyland stabilised Disney's fortune and allowed

more expansion into family live action films such as *Old Yeller* and *Mary Poppins*. Disney continued to expand with syndicated TV presentations *The Wonderful World of Disney*, *Mickey Mouse Club* and eventually the Disney Channel. Disney was not only an American icon; America became Disney's icon.

Disney had been a chain smoker all his adult life but was careful not to be photographed or seen by children smoking. After some corrective surgery on his neck, malignant lung cancer was discovered and his left lung was removed. Surgeons explained he had little time left and on December 15 1966, at the age of 65, Disney died of acute circulatory collapse.

Legend has it that he was cryogenically frozen and his remains buried beneath the Pirates of the Caribbean ride – to be 'reanimated' in the future. His ashes in fact are interred at Forest Lawn Memorial Park in Glendale, California.

He was a man that made his dreams come true, created a fantasyland that we can, all for a moment, inhabit. All generated from the dreams of a young boy who had most of his dreams stolen as a child, with his only childhood pet being a squeaky black mouse.

Walt Disney

JUDY GARLAND
(1922–1969)

FERNCLIFF CEMETERY,
HARTSDALE, NEW YORK, USA

There is no more callous example of the exploitation of talent than the story of Frances Ethel Gumm. Born on June 10, 1922 into a theatrical family, young Judy Garland, as she would be later known, performed with her sisters at the age of two at her parents Grand Rapids theatre. Her family relocated after a scandal involving her father and young male ushers and made their home in California where Mrs Ethel Gumm went about getting her daughters into pictures.

The Gumm Sisters (they changed their name to the Garland Sisters in 1934) appeared in a variety of short features, their singing winning them constant but small time work in vaudeville and movie shorts. The act broke up in 1935 when Suzy Garland ran off with Lee Kahn, a member of the Jimmy Davis orchestra, but not before movie director Busby Berkeley saw them at the Orpheum. Judy was signed to MGM at age 13. She was schooled with other stars and soon felt inferior about her looks (Lana Turner and Elizabeth Taylor were at the school), a disposition that dogged her throughout her life. This was exacerbated by the

181

studio playing down her appearance for the girl next door roles that defined her.

A string of co-starring roles with Mickey Rooney showed Garland her niche, her beautiful singing voice and her hesitant, unsure persona clicked with the audience and stardom came quickly. It was during this time, to maintain her tight performance and appearance schedules, that she was supplied with amphetamines and barbiturates, which were rumoured to have come from studio heads. This started an addiction that would lead to her professional and physical demise.

Cast in *The Wizard of Oz*, Garland had graduated from co-star to star and was MGM's most bankable star of the late 1930s. It was in this era that she recorded her most successful songs, 'Over the Rainbow', 'The Trolley Song', 'On the Atchison, Topeka and Santa Fe', all featuring in a series of equally successful musicals – *Easter Parade* and *Meet Me in St Louis*. She seemed to have successfully transitioned from child actor to adult super star. However, her growing addiction and problems in her personal life were ever present.

Her heart was broken when her lover Artie Shaw eloped with Lana Turner. Garland went on to wed musician David Rose and was divorced three years later, then in 1945 she married Vincente Minnelli with whom she had her first child, Liza, in 1946. They divorced six years later. Her first suicide attempt came in 1947, and stints in psychiatric hospitals followed. Her appearance on set was often late or non-existent – a pattern which began after a failed dramatic role in *The Clock*. She was abusing alcohol as well as using opioid tablets, barbiturates and amphetamines to overcome her insecurities and maintain work schedules. Her successes continued but by the early 1950s she was being replaced on films or suspended from contracts – she split with MGM after 15 years.

Garland went back to the stage to reinvigorate her career. Her stage appearances were enormous successes. In 1952 she married Sid Luft and had two children, her existence stabilised somewhat. She returned to film to make *A Star is Born*, the plot shadowed Garland's career and the film was an enormous success, but in a sense this was her swansong. Garland's films after this were largely dramatic and old demons continued to haunt her after she failed to win the Oscar for what she considered was a defining performance in *A Star is Born*.

Judy Garland

She performed in TV galas and on stage, but by 1959 she had been hospitalised with acute hepatitis. After recovering she pushed hard for success in TV but her show was cancelled in 1964 and she was personally, financially and emotionally devastated. Her final years were marked by stage performances oscillating between brilliant and shameful. She accumulated two more husbands – Mark Herron and Mickey Deans. She married Deans three months before her death.

She was found dead in her Chelsea home on June 22 1969. The cause was barbiturate poisoning; an accidental death was ruled but her coroner noted her health was so poor that little time was left for her. Her body was taken to New York for a memorial service and an estimated 20,000 lined the route in Manhattan. She was interred in a crypt in the mausoleum of Ferncliff Cemetery, New York.

A life loved and abused, Judy Garland became an icon for those who found themselves exploited, but there are few who had suffered so much at the hands of others and the demands of talent as Garland did in her lifetime.

Judy Garland

ROCK HUDSON
(1925–1985)

FOREST LAWN CEMETERY,
CATHEDRAL CITY, CALIFORNIA,
USA

The most successful leading man of the 1950s and 60s and one of the first stars to feel the pressure of TV on his career, Rock Hudson's career was overshadowed by being the first major star to succumb to AIDS. He was also the first to publicly admit the illness, albeit belatedly, but facing consequences and changing the perception of the illness in Hollywood and around the world.

Hudson was born Roy Harold Scherer Jr. on November 17, 1925, the son of a mechanic and telephonist Katherine Wood. Hudson had an unremarkable childhood but felt the pain of the Depression when his father abandoned the family. His mother remarried and her new husband, Wally Fitzgerald, adopted Hudson. Academically weak, Hudson sang in his school choir and worked as a caddy.

He served in the Philippines in World War II in the navy and in 1946 moved to LA to break into movies. He was taken on by agent Henry Willson because of his looks

and changed his name to Rock Hudson. He landed a single line in the film *Fighter Squadron* (where he took 38 takes to deliver the line). Willson had him thoroughly coached but he struggled to remember lines throughout his career. Magazine and TV commercials kept him in the public eye until 1954 when he starred in *Magnificent Obsession*, directed by Douglas Sirk. He went on to immense popularity with *Giant* in 1956, when he was nominated for an Oscar. Sirk became a father figure to Hudson and the pair made nine successful films together.

Hudson moved into romantic comedies in the 1960s, starring alongside Doris Day, and his popularity soared. These films became his signature but as tastes changed dramatically the end of the decade saw Hudson struggling for popularity, despite critically acclaimed performances in films such as *Seconds* (1966) and *Ice Station Zebra* (1968) Hudson was one of the biggest stars to move into TV and the series *Macmillan & Wife* was a long running success but other factors were imposing themselves onto Hudson's life. Heavy drinking and smoking saw Hudson suffer a heart attack in 1981 requiring multiple bypass surgery. His recovery was slow, his appearance was gaunt and his voice changed, causing his character to be written out of *Dynasty*. It was rumoured that liver cancer was the problem but the realities of Hudson's personal life were the root cause.

Hudson had long been the focus of rumoured homosexuality. His managers had taken preventative actions by marrying him to Henry Willson's secretary, Phyllis Gates. The marriage lasted three years. In fact, Hudson had long-term relationships with several men and many other liaisons (according to Giant co-star Elizabeth Taylor, one was with James Dean). Trying to publicly maintain his screen persona as a romantic lead, the reality was that Hudson had been diagnosed with HIV in 1984. Hudson's deteriorating appearance fuelled speculation and he travelled to the American Hospital in Paris to seek treatment. On July 25, 1985 his publicist confirmed that Hudson had AIDS. On his return to LA he was taken from the plane on a stretcher and flown by helicopter UCLA Medical centre. He was released after a month to return to his home, 'The Castle' in Beverly Hills, where he died on October 2, 1985. Hudson requested no funeral, his body was cremated hours after his death and a cenotaph was established at Forest Lawn Cemetery. Hudson's trials gave a face to the disease and although the stigma

remained the public perception of homosexuality began to shift. His long-term partners, Marc Christian and Tom Clark, fought protracted legal cases about his estate and 'intentional infliction of emotional distress' changed Californian law. Secrecy over his personal life and secrecy between lovers dogged his existence, in life and after.

Rock Hudson

JAMES CAGNEY
(1899–1986)

GATE OF HEAVEN CEMETERY,
HAWTHORNE, NEW YORK, USA

Born on the tough streets of New York, a child of the roaring twenties and then the Depression, James Cagney Jr. brought to the screen the layered gangster and the light hearted dancer with equal aplomb. His unique style and characterisation embedded him in popular culture and assured his status. Recognised in the top ten box office draw cards for more than 30 years – he is one of the most revered figures amongst his colleagues, an unlikely but superbly talented screen legend.

James Cagney Jr. was born on the lower east side in 1899 into an Irish family struggling with the horrors of poverty (two of his siblings died in infancy). A sickly child, but very intelligent – he went to Columbia College but dropped out after the death of his father – he went on to hold a succession of odd jobs while supporting his family. Hardened and pugilistic, he was runner up at New York State Lightweight boxing title but was prevented from continuing by his mother. He became exposed to film at Vitagraph Studios, standing in for his brother

when he became ill. His photographic memory meant he knew all the rehearsal positions for everyone. He had learnt to dance from observation and could see the potential of money making in the busy vaudeville and film scene. Cagney then progressed to Broadway and landed a part in the musical *Pitter Patter*. Here he met his wife 'Billie' Vernon and they married in 1922. The vagaries of seeking work sent Cagney and Vernon to California in 1924. Cagney set up a dance studio to make ends meet but eventually the couple moved back to New York. For the next four years, Cagney went back to vaudeville and Broadway, with varied success, struggles, and disappointment along the way. Eventually Cagney secured a film lead opposite Joan Blondell in 1930, *Sinner's Holiday*, playing a complex bad guy who becomes a killer, a characterisation that would become Cagney's signature piece. The role led to a seven-year contract at $400 a week, at the height of the Depression. Barely a year later, Cagney made *The Public Enemy*, in a role shocked and intrigued audiences, particularly the violence towards his co-star, Mae Clark. The film was an enormous financial success. The gangster genre had been born. Astute, Cagney realised that the studios were making enormous, guaranteed profit and began his campaign for better pay – a quirk that would see him become notorious amongst studio heads. His campaign against Warner Bros. was ongoing and saw him walk out on contracts only to return with much better conditions. The $400 a week had turned into $150,000 a film.

Cagney's roles started to broaden and he played George M. Cohan in *Yankee Doodle Dandy* (his personal favourite), a very successful biopic that allowed him to dance and act without the restrictions of genre. Cagney was heavily involved in supporting service men and toured widely between 1942 and 1945. His pugnacity drew him into confrontations (he took a stand against the use of live ammunition on set). It was at this time he was accused of communist sympathies for his support of an anti-Nazi league, but Cagney's strength of character and profile shook off the accusations. He took on the Presidency of the Screen Actors Guild to ward off growing Mafia influence in the industry. It was rumoured that the mafia would stage an accident on set as a warning but his friend, George Raft, allegedly intervened on his behalf.

After several stints in independent production, Cagney returned to Warner

James Cagney

Bros. to make the gangster film *White Heat* in 1949. A critically celebrated role quickly followed with the Academy Award nominated, *Love Me or Leave Me*. Cagney continued to make films outside the genre, often depicting servicemen but his output slowed. He retired from the screen in 1961 to his farm in Stanfordville, Dutchess County, New York to indulge his hobby of painting and his interest in agriculture and horses.

Cagney returned to the screen on occasion between 1977 and 1984, largely to aid in his recovery from a stroke but his fragility reduced these appearances to cameos.

Cagney died at his Verney Farm, named after his wife who died on Easter Sunday, 1986. President Ronald Reagan gave his funeral oration and his pallbearers were boxer Floyd Patterson and dancer Mikhail Baryshnikov. He rests at Cemetery of the Gate of Heaven in Hawthorne, New York. Cagney was the epitome of the American dream of making it big in Hollywood, an extraordinary talent and a man true to himself.

James Cagney

FRANK SINATRA
(1915–1998)

DESERT MEMORIAL PARK,
CATHEDRAL CITY, CALIFORNIA,
USA

The first singer to capture the teenage market and widely regarded as the finest popular singer of the twentieth century, Francis Albert Sinatra stood over the popular music scene for forty years. Defying trends and amassing a fortune, 'Old Blue Eyes' became his own unmistakable brand.

Frank Sinatra was born on December 12, 1915, the only child of Italian immigrants Antonio Sinatra and Natalina Garaventa in Hoboken, New Jersey. A brash and uncontrolled child, Sinatra left school without graduating, attending only 47 days of high school before being expelled for rowdy behaviour. He had already been singing in bars from age eight. He held a succession of 'nothing' jobs before singing professionally in the 1930s with the Hoboken Four, winning a talent quest and a six-month contract to perform across the US.

Sinatra would come to perfect his craft when Harry James, the acclaimed big band leader, hired him on a one-year contract. James taught Sinatra how to sing

professionally – developing his technique and familiarising him with music theory. His big break came when he signed with Tommy Dorsey, an even bigger star who bound Sinatra into a contract that took one third of Sinatra's lifetime earnings. His recordings with Dorsey targeted a new audience – 'bobby soxers' – teenage girls. It was Sinatra's appeal to this market that guaranteed his success. An estimated 35,000 fans were turned away from a 1944 Paramount Theatre performance. A musician's strike in 1942–44 ironically consolidated Sinatra's status – no new recordings were made but live radio performances were exempt. Sinatra signed with Columbia Records in 1943 and for the remainder of the 40s Sinatra became a star. His crossed over into film, (*Anchors Aweigh*, *Take Me Out to the Ball Game*) and still maintained a profile on radio, TV and advertising. However, by 1950 Sinatra felt his star was waning as he moved into his thirties.

His performance in *From Here to Eternity*, and a change in direction in song choice and recording (*In the Wee Small Hours*), saved Sinatra's career. His connection with one of the finest musical arrangers of the era, Nelson Riddle, produced his biggest hits. Other connections began to emerge in the 50s and 60s – the long rumoured associations with organised crime figures, most notably Sam Giancana, and Carlo Gambino, began to haunt Sinatra. He exploited these connections in his appearances in Las Vegas and never denied his friendships, a persona he utilised in his 'Rat Pack' days with Dean Martin, Sammy Davis Jr. and Peter Lawford in the early 1960s. His attitude to life was epitomised in his song 'My Way' and he was courted by his controversial behaviour and total irreverence for the press. He caused nationwide strikes on his Australian Tour in 1974 (after calling female journalists 'hookers') and played at Sun City in 1981 in opposition to the world wide apartheid boycott. He was paid two million dollars for the gig.

Sinatra had moved into retirement in the 1970s, recording his last studio album for Reprise Records (his label). Always a vicious critic of rock and roll and counterculture, he was forced to record some new tracks in an attempt to remain relevant but his strength remained with crooner music and big band-arranged ballads. He made comebacks and recorded intermittently, and when his film career faded he traded on the reverence and appreciation shown to him across generations but his appearance became less frequent in the 1990s.

Sinatra had married three times, most famously to actress Ava Gardner, and had three children from his first marriage. He had been a strong Democrat supporter until he was snubbed by Kennedy in 1962, as JFK distanced himself from Mafia connections. Despite his agnostic views, he became Catholic as his health began to fail, famously donating to the Church as he became ill.

He died on May 14, 1998 of a heart attack at the age of 82 with third wife Barbara Marx by his side. From the brash young boy to the uncertain and anxious young man on the way up, Sinatra was the uncompromising statesman of music whose talent outshone all others in the entertainment world.

Frank Sinatra

JOHN WAYNE
(1907–1979)

PACIFIC VIEW MEMORIAL PARK, NEWPORT BEACH, ORANGE COUNTY, CALIFORNIA, USA

Star of over a 170 films, icon of the frontier myth, fanatical chess player and the top box office draw for three decades – John Wayne left his birth name (Marion Robert Morrison) far behind. By the end of his life, cut short by lung cancer, Wayne had come to symbolise America for a generation of movie goers, politicians and the wider world.

Born in Iowa but soon relocated to greater LA, Wayne graduated from Glendale High School to USC on a football scholarship before a surfing accident ended his football career. Wayne found himself working as a prop boy on silent movie sets to pay for his pre law studies and quickly moved on to bit parts. He was physically imposing and was cast in *The Big Trail* (1930) in a starring role. His persona, his drawl, his distinctive walk (modelled on Wyatt Earp, a figure around the sets of Hollywood at the time) and his stage name was set. His career began with 'poverty row' films (low budget westerns known as 'horse operas') and he appeared in 80 films during this time until his breakthrough role in John Ford's *Stagecoach*

in 1939. Ford thought that's Wayne's appeal as an 'everyman' would make him a huge star.

The onset of World War II created a problem for Wayne, considered the epitome of masculinity he failed to serve (he was already the father of four children and holding out for a possible commission, he was eventually held back by studios). This issue dogged him for the remainder of his life, which explains the patriotic stand her took on political issues both on and off screen.

Wayne spent the most creative and successful two decades of his career featuring in John Ford's epic westerns where he honed his conflicted, but supremely moral hero, most clearly presented in *The Searchers* (1956). He also portrayed soldiers (*The Sands of Iwo Jima*, in 1949, which brought him his first Academy Award nomination) and aviators (*Island in the Sky*, 1953) in a series of films that confirmed his status in the public eye and reinforced his right wing politics. Some, notably, *Green Berets* (1968) flew in the face of public opinion and Wayne's popularity suffered as America became the focal point for counterculture activities in the 60s. His political support for US President Richard Nixon showed him at odds with younger audiences but the fact that he won the Oscar for *True Grit* (1969) shows the high esteem in which the film industry held him.

Wayne's last film was *The Shootist* (1976), where he portrayed a man dying of cancer, which was poignant as this was Wayne's situation at the time.

He was a five packet a day man, drank heavily and was married three times, all to women of Hispanic descent (he also had long running affairs with Marlene Dietrich and Merle Oberon). He was very well-liked and respected by his film associates largely because his on screen persona and his personality were so close. He also brought his battle with cancer into the public forum and discussed it with grace and courage. He succumbed on June 11, 1979 to stomach cancer. It is interesting to note that Wayne starred in *The Conqueror* (1956), a film shot in Nevada, downwind of nuclear testing, which saw many members of the cast and crew struck down with some sort of cancer.

His legacy remains in the many, many monuments – airports, statues, schools, mosaics, highways, foundations and remarkable financial success – but his resting place bears a simple plaque and was, for many years unmarked. It now

features his quote about the nature of tomorrow: 'It comes into us at midnight very clean. It puts itself in our hands....hopes we've learned something from yesterday,' and the Spanish epitaph 'Feo, fuerte y formal' (formal, strong and ugly). Few people earn iconic status in their lifetime, but testament to Wayne's enormous status was Japan's Emperor Hirohito's wish to meet John Wayne on his visit to the US in 1975. Wayne remained a symbol of the nation that had defeated Japan in World War II.

John Wayne

LUCILLE BALL
(1911–1989)

LAKE VIEW CEMETERY,
JAMESTOWN, NEW YORK, USA

The most successful TV sitcom actress of all time and a pioneer in the creation of television production worldwide, Lucille Ball was the antithesis of her on scene persona. Adept and astute in business, and discerning in her professional and personal life, she was so loved by her audience that a single episode out-rated the inauguration of President Eisenhower in 1957 by 15 million viewers.

Lucille Désirée Ball was born August 6, 1911 to Henry Ball and De Hunt in Celeron Jamestown, New York. Her father, a linesman for Bell Telephone died of typhoid when she was four and she spent much of her childhood in the care of her eccentric grandparents until her mother remarried. Her stepfather came from a puritanical Swedish family and Ball stayed in the care of her step grandparents who forbade mirrors – for the sake of vanity. Lucille's childhood see-sawed from abandon to control until she began to dance onstage for Church functions.

When Lucille 14, her mother had scrapped together enough funds to have her

sent to drama school in New York (she was concerned with Lucille's relationship with a local boy aged 23) but Ball despised drama school. She later said that, 'all I learned at drama school was to be frightened' and she returned home.

Determined to prove the drama school wrong she returned to New York and became a successful model but became ill with rheumatic fever and was ill for two years. Work was sporadic for her in New York in 1932, and in 1933 she moved to LA and picked up a series of B-grade films throughout the 30s. She was signed to MGM in the 40s and was dubbed 'Queen of the B's'. She supplemented her income with radio work and her comedic strength developed on the back of a radio wacky wife character she and her Cuban husband Desi Arnaz worked up an act they toured successfully. This became the genesis for the *I Love Lucy* show for CBS. Her TV dynasty had begun and she established many ground-breaking elements for TV. Ball was the first female head of a TV production company, multiple cameras were used, the show was filmed before a live audience and sets were adjacent and distinct. *I Love Lucy* dominated TV in the fifties and DESILU productions went on to produce *The Untouchables*, *Star Trek* and *Mission: Impossible*.

Ball and Arnaz had eloped in 1940 and she had always tried to disguise that her husband was six years younger than her'. They had met while filming and stayed together until 1960. The spark that made the comedy work so well had its seed in Arnaz's chaotic life as a bandleader and Ball's attempt to keep up with him and his drinking. She first sought a divorce in 1944 but changed her mind and the birth of two children held the marriage together until the 'nightmare' (her expression) had to end. They divorced in 1960, and she later commented that the reality of their life together was nothing like their TV show.

Variations of *I Love Lucy* with Gale Gordon (*The Lucy Show, Here's Lucy*) ran until 1974 under the direction of her new husband Garry Morton (who was 13 years her junior). This partnership, both business and professional, ran for the rest of her life. Ball was one of the very few actors to be called before the House Committee on Un-American Activities and remain unscathed. She admitted an affiliation with the Communist Party in her youth but excused her behaviour as being controlled by her eccentric grandfather and she was exonerated. It also helped that FBI head J. Edgar Hoover loved her show.

Lucille Ball

Always happy to be the self-deprecating clown she explained that she wasn't funny, she was brave.

Lucy died on April 26, 1989 after complications from heart surgery, a weakness that she had acquired after her bout of rheumatic fever as a young, starving actress in New York. Her ashes were interred at Forest Lawn Cemetery but in 2002 were moved to Jamestown, New York, to be with her grandparents, parents and brother.

Lucille Ball

DEAN MARTIN
(1917–1995)

WESTWOOD MEMORIAL PARK,
LOS ANGELES, CALIFORNIA, USA

From a poor Italian background, with broken English and a hard knuckle introduction into show business, Dean Martin emerged as an enduring and popular entertainer. Working in film, TV, music recording and on stage simultaneously endeared himself to audiences world-wide for more than three decades.

Dean Martin was born on June 7, 1917 in Steubenville, Ohio to an Abruzzan immigrant family. He did not speak English until he attended school at age five. Bullied at school because of his background, he was disinterested in school and left at age 15 to work as a bootlegger, a croupier at an illegal casino, a blackjack dealer, a mill worker and boxer. As 'Kid Crochet' he lost 11 of 12 fights but made money on the side by charging punters to bet on bare-knuckle fights he staged in his apartment.

He began singing with Ernie Mckay's Orchestra as a crooner, but unable to compete with the likes of Sinatra he remained an East Coast nightclub crooner until he met comedian Jerry Lewis in 1946 at the Glass Hat in New York. Here they

put together a musical-comedy act based on adlibbing and playing off each other, which became enormously popular. The duo went from clubs in Atlantic City to Broadway success, attracting thousands of fans who clambered for tickets to their sold out shows. A pop phenomenon in the 1940s, Martin and Lewis were hired for comic relief in the film, *My Friend Irma* (1949) and this appearance catapulted them into film stardom.

Martin was never comfortable with his straight man role but the pairing was very lucrative and he stayed with it for 10 years to the day before a very acrimonious split. Martin wanted 'dramatic gravitas' and a string of films (*Some Came Running, The Young Lions* and *Rio Bravo*) saw him excel in strong dramatic roles. He eventually returned to light comedy in 1960s, and took on spoof roles parodying his boozy persona in a series of 'Rat Pack' films with Frank Sinatra as well as the lucrative 'Matt Helm' spy movies.

He was still active in the recording industry, releasing more than 600 songs in his lifetime (his 1964 hit 'Everybody Loves Somebody Sometime' even knocked The Beatles off the top of the charts). This also drove his night club career, and he appeared for three decades in Las Vegas featuring shows with the 'Rat Pack' friends perfecting their collective hard-drinking, gambling and partying persona. Martin exploited his image to launch a successful TV career, playing off his drunken and inappropriate remarks but in a harmless, charming way. His *Dean Martin Show* had a loose format (apparently Martin rarely showed for rehearsals) featuring friends from his nightclub acts and adlibbed comedy. This morphed into a series of celebrity 'roasts' in the 1970s, which still remain an important Hollywood tradition. Martin's show ran for nine years and helped him survive the counterculture revolution in the US. When the show was cancelled in 1974, Martin's career went back to Las Vegas and slowly into retirement.

He had married three times and produced seven children who were all attached to show business, largely through Martin's connections or companies. For someone who was known for his emotional aloofness, the death of his son Dean Paul Martin in an air crash in 1987 hastened Martin's demise. Diagnosed with lung cancer, he died on December 25, 1995 aged 78.

'Dino' was that rare person who made a career out of being himself – whether

Dean Martin

it was struggling to find identity and recognition in the 1940s or parodying himself in the 70s. An archetype of the Las Vegas entertainer – that was his role in life as he say it, to entertain.

Chapter Seven

CRIMINALS

KING RICHARD III
(1452–1485)

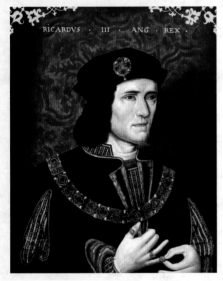

RICARDVS · III · ANG · REX ·

GREYFRIARS CHURCH LEICESTER (BENEATH THE CHOIR), REBURIAL AT LEICESTER CATHEDRAL, ENGLAND, 2015

Richard Plantagenet, King of England, last Plantagenet king, last English King to be killed in battle and last on British soil. Maligned? Monster? King for only two years, Richard's legacy far outweighs the length of his reign. The manner of his death is the stuff of literature and legend, as was his reign. His body has given up secrets that have rattled the Monarchy and its legitimacy. With the death of Richard came the end of the Middle Ages and the Tudors distinguishing themselves as monarchs of the English Renaissance. His end on Bosworth Field in some ways marked the end of the barbarism that was associated with England and the English monarchs.

When Richard's brother, King Edward IV died, he was named Lord Protector of the Realm for Edward's successor, Edward V, only 12 years old at the time. Richard escorted his nephew to the Tower of London to await his coronation, joined shortly afterwards by Edward's younger brother. Richard had contrived to have his nephews declared illegitimate and so Edward's claim on the throne was invalid. The following day a parliament was called and lords and commoners validated Richard's claims. Richard III began his reign the following day. The boys were never seen in public again. The Princes in the Tower, it was assumed, had been murdered on Richard's orders.

Richard had spent many of his formative years embroiled in the Wars of the Roses and the intrigues and turmoil of a country racked by decades of civil war. He contracted idiopathic scoliosis in adolescence and his skeleton was misshapen, however it likely did not cause any major physical deformity that could not be disguised by clothing, his deformity may have played a part in developing his psychology. He had connived the accumulation of large estates through his association and marriage to Anne Neville. He had distinguished himself in battle in the wars against France and Scotland and controlled the North of England as Lord Protector for Edward IV. But rebellions soon erupted against Richard, fuelled by disaffected nobles and where the first rebellion failed, the second in 1485, led by Henry Tudor brought the opposing armies together on Bosworth Field. Betrayed on the field and isolated from his forces, Richard charged at Henry but was cut down by Welsh infantry, a hauberk slicing through the back of Richard's skull before he was set upon.

The manner of his death was confirmed when his remains were found in 2012 at the site of Greyfriars Church in Leicester. The body revealed the death blow and seven others to the skull, indicating that Richard had lost his helmet. Other wounds confirm the humiliation given to Richard's body after death, his body then stripped and thrown across a horse. He was hastily buried in Greyfriars and a covering stone was visible up till 1612.

Richard's remains throw up another startling fact. DNA testing through his maternal antecedents confirmed Richard's identity but his paternal DNA casts doubt on the line of English kings, affecting claims to the throne. After much debate and legal wrangling the remains of the king were interred in Leicester Cathedral in the spring of 2015.

Humiliated in death and vilified in literature and by historians, Richard's distorted body gives us a view of a man of his times – hardened, shaped by war and

intrigue – and so takes his place amongst royalty, giving a reminder of its origins and its nature.

NED KELLY
(1854–1880)

GRETA CEMETERY, VICTORIA, AUSTRALIA

Folk hero or lawless, shabby professional criminal? 'Ned' Kelly seems to fit the mould of so many heroes of the 19th century. His image wavers between the lionising of his actions by a distant and admiring public in a fight against colonial oppression or a callous and brutal thug who perpetrated crimes for the single purpose of wealth. The facts waver too; confessions are dubious, witnesses self-serving and accusers unreliable. There is however no doubt that Kelly's 'truth' tells us more about the Australian psyche than anything else.

Born in 1854 at Beveridge in colonial Victoria to Red (John) Kelly and Ellen Quinn. His father was an Irish prisoner who had settled in Victoria after serving his sentence for theft in Van Diemen's Land where he had established himself as an expert cattle thief. Young Ned Kelly was shaped by some fundamental incidents in his childhood; the first being the death of his father after a stretch in prison for theft that left Ned as the eldest of eight children and the family indigent. Mrs Kelly moved the family close to her family connections near Greta in Victoria. Her family

were well known to police and her subsequent marriage to George King (a horse thief) embedded young Ned in a web of criminality. The targets were wealthy graziers and their agents, the police.

Ned's first documented crime was 'highway robbery'. He stole money from a Chinese trader but as with many of Ned's crimes the evidence was thin or manipulated. Ned habitually denied responsibility, intimidated and lied – as did his family in criminal matters. This drew the ire of the local constabulary who took personal dislikes to the Kellys. He soon fell in with Harry Power, a bushranger, and learned the trade but Power was captured in 1870 and Ned was released after a month when no evidence could be found. However, summary offences soon became the serious charge of horse stealing and Ned was sentenced to three years in Melbourne's Pentridge Prison.

Soon after his release the second fundamental event of Ned's life occurred. A drunken trooper, Fitzpatrick, attended the Kelly's home and tried to arrest Dan Kelly. The facts cannot be established but Ned was accused of attempted murder and escaped, his mother was charged with aiding and abetting, and imprisoned. Ned went on the run with his brother Dan, Steve Hart and Joe Byrne. The constabulary sent Sgt Kennedy, Constables Lonigan, Scanlon and McIntyre to apprehend the outlaws. At Stringybark Creek the Kelly Gang surprised McIntyre guarding the camp and murdered the other men. McIntyre escaped and the Victorian government proclaimed them as outlaws. Their fate was sealed.

The Kelly Gang developed a new methodology; bank robbery done without threat to local people, who were detained and then released, an act that garnered the 'Robin Hood' image for Ned. The first instance was at Faithfull Creek (near Euroa) – locking up 22 while they robbed the National Bank. Then at Jerilderie, they took possession of the police station, took uniforms and held up the New South Wales Bank, holding 60 people in the Royal Hotel next door. Here Kelly gave a bank teller an 8000 word 'Jerilderie' letter that justified his behaviour and claimed the government was engaged in a race war against Irish Catholics.

They struck next at Glenrowan, trying to derail a currency train. They held 60 people captive in the local hotel but released Thomas Curnow, his wife and child who alerted authorities. The gang had come prepared with armour; Ned's weighed

Ned Kelly

41 kilograms, including a cylindrical head piece and body plates but critically, no coverage of his legs. The police surrounded the hotel and mortally wounded Joe Byrne. Ned escaped into the bush but returned in early morning and was taken down by gunfire. Most innocents had escaped and the police set fire to the hotel; burning Dan Kelly and Steve Hart to death.

Ned was tried for the murder of Constable Lonigan at Stringy Bark Creek and sentenced to be hanged, the sentence was carried out on November 11, 1880.

'Such is life.' was Kelly's comment whilst being led to his execution and, 'so it has come to this' purportedly his last words. Kelly's remains were finally laid to rest, at Greta near Glenrowan after long years in an unmarked grave in Old Melbourne gaol then Pentridge Prison. A piece of his skull was interred, the rest taken as a trophy (at one time found in a safe in Canberra but now missing).

Kelly's place in Australian tradition is difficult but undeniable – revisionists see him as self-centred and callous criminal, his life deluded and at times cruel and farcical. His legend is that of the epitome of underdog, (a petition of 30,000 signatures pleaded for mercy) a symbol of the common man whose only path is rebellion against forces that create cruelty and injustice. Whatever the truth, Kelly sits in the Australian psyche and that we must accept.

Ned Kelly

JESSE JAMES
(1847–1882)

MOUNT OLIVET CEMETERY,
KEARNEY, CLAY COUNTY,
MISSOURI, USA

No other individual explores the difference in perceptions generated in the US – hero or villain than Jesse Woodson James.

Born on September 5, 1847, Jesse accumulated a long list of titles in a brutal career; outlaw, gang leader, guerrilla, bushwhacker, train robber and murderer. He was born into a civilised and educated family at a time in American history when the rule of law was questioned and violence was a mainstay of existence. His father died when Jesse was three, ministering to prospectors in the Californian Gold Rush, after his father's death his mother remarried twice. Her third husband, Reuben Samuel, established a successful tobacco plantation in Missouri.

The approach of the Civil War reshaped Jesse's life. His older brother Frank had served in the local militia and introduced Jesse to secessionist 'jaywalkers' or 'bushwhackers', rural guerrillas who killed Union supporters and forces, often scalping their victims to terrify. The result was Union forces attacking

homesteads. The James' home was attacked and the boys' stepfather, Reuben Samuel was tortured (hanged briefly) and Jesse lashed. Jesse's brother Frank was involved in the Lawrence massacre in Kansas (200 men and boys murdered) in 1863. The following year they were involved in the Centralia massacre, killing 22 unarmed Union troops where Jesse was severely wounded.

The end of the Civil War saw the James gang evolve into a criminal enterprise. They carried out the first peacetime bank robbery in 1866, the beginning of their decade long criminal history. The first of many innocent bystanders was shot (Jesse claimed 14 murders) and claimed that their string of robberies was aimed at local Union supporters who had profiteered from the war. Jesse's individual fame (or infamy) came in 1869, when robbing Davies County Savings, he shot and killed the cashier believing him to be an enemy from the Civil War. Their daring escape from the posse added to the legend and Jesse was declared an outlaw for the first time and Governor Crittenden of Missouri set a reward for capture. Jesse wrote to the press and his letters were published. They asserted his innocence and became increasingly political, and the gang continued their robberies – holding up baggage cars in trains, daylight attacks on fairs hammed up for the audience – wearing KKK masks to assert their Confederate status.

They ranged from Texas to Iowa, their 'Robin Hood' image enhanced by secret support from Southern sympathisers and they continued to elude the Pinkerton Detective Agency, several agents of which they killed. Allan Pinkerton sought to use guerrilla tactics against the James family and he bombed the farm on January 1875, killing Jesse's half-brother and mutilating Zerelda James, Jesse's mother. Their status rose and they were on the verge of being given an amnesty when another robbery in Minnesota saw only Jesse and Frank survive – two more innocent victims were killed.

Jesse and Frank now took on 'rubes' (inexperienced criminals) to supplement the loss of the gang and it was two brothers, Robert and Charley Ford that would eventually kill Jesse. Frank had disappeared in Tennessee, laying low and Jesse had taken on the identity of Thomas Howard (even his wife Zee and children knew him as Tom) but Jesse's paranoia was beginning to bite. It was suspected that he murdered some gang members (a sardonic joke was never to let Jesse get behind

Jesse James

you) and was intending to murder the Ford brothers who had moved into his house in preparation for the next robbery.

Jesse and the Fords had breakfasted when Jesse, who had taken his jacket and guns off due to the heat, had stood on chair to straighten a picture and was shot in the back of the head by Robert Ford. It was April 3, 1882. The Ford brothers were indicted for murder but pardoned two hours later. Robert had been in secret negotiations with Governor Crittenden to kill Jesse.

Jesse's body was displayed and photographed, stored on ice to satisfy the demand and curiosity. The Ford brothers toured the West, re-enacting the death of Jesse James. Three years later Charley Ford, tuberculoid and morphine addicted, took his own life. Edward O'Kelley shot Robert nine years later in his saloon in Colorado. O'Kelley was pardoned by the governor.

James was interred on the James Family Farm, his body later moved to Kearney, Clay County, Missouri. His epitaph written by his mother states 'My beloved son, murdered by a Traitor and Coward whose name is not worthy to appear here'.

Perception and reality were at odds for Jesse James and his those who loved and feared him.

Jesse James

WYATT EARP
(1848–1929)

HILLS OF ETERNITY MEMORIAL
PARK, COLMA, CALIFORNIA, USA

No name evokes the illusion of the Wild West more than Wyatt Earp and no other moment in the history of the West was more famous than the Gunfight at the O.K. Corral in Tombstone, Arizona. Lawman, gunfighter, gambler, buffalo hunter, prospector, saloon owner, Earp was all these things and more ... perhaps even operating outside the law of the day.

Earp was born in Illinois in 1848 and had his formative years in the Civil War. The pressure to survive in such times led his father to organise a wagon train to California and a better life but Earp and his family drifted back east and settled in Lamar, Missouri. His father became constable and Wyatt followed a year later when his father became Justice of the Peace.

Wyatt seemed to have found his niche, but with the death of his first wife and child from typhoid, Wyatt spiralled out of control and stepped to the other side of the law. He frequented brothels, and used his imposing size and fearlessness to extort money or run scams, he became known as the Peoria Bummer (a man

of low character, standover man or pimp). He headed for Wichita, a railhead town that was the epitome of the Wild West. Here, Earp gained a position in the marshal's office and dealt 'faro' at the Long Branch saloon, a pattern that would occur throughout Earp's life.

Earp headed to Dodge City to meet up with his brother James and continued his work as a lawman. Here he saved Bat Masterson's life in a standoff with some Texas 'Cowboys' (the term refers to criminals; real cattlemen were known as ranchers), and this is where he made his reputation as a lawman and gunfighter.

He and another brother, Virgil took up the opportunity to move to Tombstone in Arizona, a town booming with silver mining. His brother was the Deputy Marshal and the events in Tombstone would define the rest of his existence. Here, the Earp brothers clashed with Cowboys, headed up by the Clanton Gang, Frank Stillwell and Pete Spencer and the McLaury brothers. They made their living holding up stagecoaches, horses and silver lodes sent from the mines. A minor confrontation about stolen mules brought them into conflict and the McLaury brothers threatened to murder the Earp brothers and anyone who stood in their way. They were part of a corrupt system of local justice and political representation headed by a local sheriff Johnny Behan. This was further complicated by Wyatt Earp and Behan sharing affections for the same woman, Josephine Marcus. Earp had given beatings to some of the Cowboys and they had gathered at the O.K. Corral to make good their threat to the Earp's on Wednesday October 26, 1881.

Virgil Earp deputised Doc Holliday, and asked Wyatt and Morgan Earp to help disarm the Cowboys. At 3pm they headed towards the corral. Ike Clanton fled but Tom and Frank McLaury and Billy Clanton were killed. The contention remains whether it was cold-blooded murder or a gunfight. The locals roused to the defence of the Earps and they were found not guilty of murder although Doc Holliday was the first to fire his nickel-plated revolver. Supporters of the Cowboys started to plot their revenge and Morgan Earp was assassinated. Wyatt hunted down Frank Stilwell in Tuscon and went with Holliday and their close associates, to kill 'Indian Charlie' Cruz, 'Curly Bill' Brocious and Johnny Barnes. After this Wyatt left Arizona and the second, largely unknown phase of his life began.

He travelled through California and as far north as Alaska searching for wealth.

Gambling and running saloons, he eventually settled in Los Angeles, living off the slim profits of his prospecting and some bounty hunting. In interviews before his death, Earp said he had no regrets about the 'situation' in Tombstone and he pointed out that corruption and 'depredations' ended after he dealt with the Cowboys. He was never wounded and often spoke of a presence that had urged care and caution in his dealings with gunfighters.

He died on January 13, 1929 at the age of 80 of acute cystitis and his funeral was held on Wiltshire Boulevard, with film stars Tom Mix and William S. Hart as pallbearers. His wife Josephine had his remains cremated and secretly buried in the Jewish Hills of Eternity Cemetery, where she would join him in 1944.

It is the most visited site in the cemetery.

Wyatt Earp

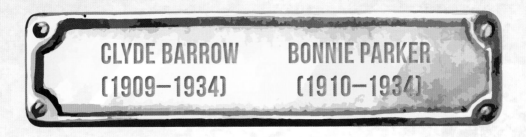

CLYDE BARROW (1909–1934)   BONNIE PARKER (1910–1934)

WESTERN HEIGHTS CEMETERY, DALLAS, TEXAS, USA, AND CROWN HILL MEMORIAL PARK, DALLAS, TEXAS, USA.

Amongst the first celebrity criminals of the modern era, the exploits of Clyde Barrow and Bonnie Parker are characterised by utter brutality, engendered by a brutal society that metered out a violent end to their lives. Their crime spree lasted for four years and the gang they headed were responsible for the murders of nine police officers, several civilians and hundreds of robberies. Their youth, their abandon, their illicit sex and the publication of photos that plainly exulted their lifestyle enhanced their reputations.

Both Parker and Barrow were children of families that were dislocated from rural society in the Depression and drifted into the vast slum area of Dallas. Bonnie Parker was an excellent student but after her marriage at the age of 15, a very different Bonnie emerged.

Clyde Barrow had an established criminal history from his early teens and was imprisoned by 1930. In prison he beat a prisoner to death who had repeatedly sexually assaulted him. Barrow was to maintain throughout his life that his motivation was to punish the Texas legal system for what happened to him at Eastham Prison Farm. This does, however, raise the implication of Barrow's ambiguous sexuality. On first meeting Parker, both were smitten and they began, with Barrow's associates, a life of professional crime focusing on gas stations and stores as robbery targets. Barrow shot a storeowner on April 30, 1932 and their criminality changed gear. On August 5, two police officers approached them in a parking lot, Barrow and associate Ray Hamilton opened fire, killing the deputy and gravely wounding the Sheriff. This was the first of nine police officers killed. W.D. Jones joined the gang and at age 16, and he and Barrow killed a young man while stealing his car. On January 6, 1933 Barrow shot and killed County Deputy Davis.

The gang were holed up at Joplin when discovered by five lawmen. Shooting their way out two more officers were killed and Barrow survived when a bullet was deflected by a suit button. The gang left behind possessions including a roll of film showing them posing with weapons, the gang became a national sensation. They rampaged north and west of Texas, the brutality of their robberies and casual killing turned public opinion sour. The gang were exploiting Federal and State boundaries to avoid capture and their daily existence became more difficult and dangerous for them and the public. Tensions within the gang heightened. Parker was badly injured in a car accident and now searching for medical assistance the gang drew attention to themselves. They were cornered in a tourist park in Arkansas and bungled a robbery but killed another officer, Marshal Humphrey and set off for Missouri. Here their suspicious behaviour (paying for meals with coins, taping newspapers over the car windows) brought a group of officers with sub machine guns, but the gang outshot the lawmen and escaped. Clyde's brother Buck, however, was fatally wounded and his sister-in-law Blanche provided the police with vital information about the gang's movements.

W.D. Jones, Parker and Clyde establish contact with their families who willingly assisted them after Parker and Clyde were both wounded in the legs. Despite

Clyde Barrow & Bonnie Parker

this, their audacity remained and they broke Ray Hamilton and Henry Methvin out of Eastham Prison Farm, bolstering their gang numbers and exacting Clyde's revenge on the Texas prison system. This pushed Federal and Texan authorities to exact their own revenge and the infamous Texas Ranger, Frank Hamer, (credited with 53 kills) was appointed Special Officer to capture the gang. They killed another two highway patrolmen and another elderly man in Oklahoma.

Hamer had figured out their *modus operandi* and laid an ambush for them in Bienville, Louisiana with a posse of six lawmen. Bonnie and Clyde were shot more than 50 times each, the lawmen emptying all their weapons as the gang's car sped past. The bodies were so badly damaged that embalming proved difficult.

Their bodies were laid separately according to the wishes of the Parker family; Bonnie rests at Crown Hill Cemetery and Clyde in Western Heights in Dallas.

Within six months of the ambush, the infamous Depression-era outlaws John Dillinger, Pretty Boy Floyd and Baby Face Nelson had all been killed. The American public had tired of the false dream of the defiant outlaw, driven by circumstances, operating beyond the law and resentful of the American way of life. The killing had become more brutal and innocent lives were claimed. Justice was done, equally brutally.

Clyde Barrow & Bonnie Parker

JOHN DILLINGER
(1903–1934)

CROWN HILL CEMETERY
INDIANAPOLIS, INDIANA, USA

A national celebrity to those down trodden by a brutal economic downslide beyond understanding and a notorious criminal to those establishing law and order in a lawless time, John Dillinger's was probably the most recognisable face in 1933 and 1934 in the American Midwest.

Born on June 22, 1903 in Oakland Indianapolis to a hard working grocer and his wife. His mother died when he was three and his stepmother married his father six years later. She resented the boy and his father beat him mercilessly to appease her and then, crippled by remorse, spoilt his son. With adolescence Dillinger's personality wavered between charming and vibrant to cruel and violent. Bullying then friendly, he was often in trouble. He left school and worked hard as a metal worker but, bored, ran wild at night to such an extent that his father moved the family to rural Mooresville. This exacerbated the boredom and trouble followed, as an escape Dillinger joined the navy. Often AWOL and in the brig he deserted and

returned to Mooresville and married his 16 year old girlfriend.

The couple moved back to Indianapolis but with no money Dillinger fell in with a local criminal and robbed a grocery store. On his father's advice he pleaded guilty and was sentence to two to 14 years in Indiana State prison. He emerged eight years later, embittered, violent and highly adept at criminality. On May 10, 1933, at the height of the Depression he robbed his first bank in Bluffton, Ohio. He was arrested in September and sent to Lima County jail. Police found a detailed escape plan on Dillinger and four days later eight of Dillinger's gang broke out of Indiana State, and using smuggled guns they shot two guards. Three of the escapees showed up at Lima and broke Dillinger out, shooting the sheriff.

Dillinger set off on his trail of bank robberies and attacks on police stations, his gang arming themselves with bulletproof vests, shotguns, pistols and rifles. In December they shot and killed a detective in Chicago, a month later they killed another while robbing the First National Bank in East Chicago. They were arrested in Arizona. Dillinger was sent to Crown Point Jail to await trial but bluffed his way out with a fake gun, took the guards' machine guns and fled into Illinois. In Chicago Dillinger teamed up with Baby Face Nelson in early 1934 for a second string of robberies and earned folk hero status. Their brazen stunts and reckless attitude to life, however, started to turn some public opinion.

In March 1934, the gang was surprised at Lincoln Court Apartments and they shot their way out. Gang member, Eddie Green, was shot dead and across town Dillinger's girlfriend was caught and arrested and sentenced to two years for harbouring a fugitive. The public's tip offs led police and the emergent FBI to Warsaw, Indiana where the gang was holed up in a summer resort. The gang shot their way out, but Nelson was separated and in stealing a car, shot another officer and wounded two others. J. Edgar Hoover ordered an all-out offensive against the gang.

In July 1934, a brothel madam, Anna Sage approached the FBI for help in avoiding deportation in exchange for information about Dillinger. The FBI accepted and on July 22, Sage, Polly Hamilton and Dillinger would go to the movies in Chicago at either the Biograph or Marbro theatres. Police were sent to both and Dillinger was spotted outside the Biograph by Agent Purvis, who lit a cigar as a

signal. Dillinger spotted the ruse and ran down an alley but was gunned down. He was pronounced dead at 10:50pm on July 22, 1934.

His death sounded the knell on the gangster era; the public tiring of would be folk heroes who were, in reality, psychopaths. Baby Face Nelson was fatally shot on November 27, and Agents Cowley and Hollis were killed.

As with all folk heroes, the end breeds myth. One myth was that Dillinger didn't die, but had placed a double at the Biograph. In reality, he was shot but he had become so desperate that he had plastic surgery to disguise himself, this had been done on the run, very painfully.

He is buried beneath layers of concrete in Crown Hill Cemetery to deter grave robbers and those that still believe him to be a hero.

John Dillinger

AL CAPONE
(1899–1947)

Mount Carmel Cemetery, Illinois, USA

Al Capone's monument in Mount Carmel Cemetery has a history of its own; imposing and austere, in stark contrast to the criminal it celebrates. Alphonse Gabriel Capone was the son of immigrant Italians, first settling in Brooklyn, New York. This was where Capone first began to learn his vicious trade. Running with gangs, notably the Five Points Gang, Capone started as a bouncer and barman. It was in a Brooklyn nightclub that he was slashed across the face and became 'Scarface', a nickname he loathed, but one which would ensure his notoriety in popular culture ever since.

Capone's career was, however, shaped in Chicago. Mentored by Johnny Torrio, Capone murdered crime boss 'Big Jim' Colosimo on Torrio's orders and the fight to control bootlegging and destroy the influence of other gangs began. After an attempt on Torrio's life, Johnny handed the reins to Capone, the most crucial event in his life. This brought Capone into direct conflict with Bugs Moran's North Side gang and the St Valentine's Day Massacre that eventuated was the beginning of the end of Capone.

Capone's career was based on corruption and violence. His sway over the Chicago police and his mutually beneficial relationship with Republican mayor, William Hale Thompson, saw unprecedented destruction of law and order. In one instance Capone's bomber, James Belcastro and four others shot a mayoral candidate, Octavius Granady, in the street on polling day; the four co-accused were policemen. All were acquitted. Capone ran the city.

Capone's folk hero appeal was carefully calculated. He claimed he was only 'providing a service to the people' by bootlegging, he was cheered at sporting events and dressed sharply, smoking cigars while distributing largess to the unemployed. His grip on the imagination of Chicago began to wane with the St Valentine's Day Massacre. Gang members, dressed in police uniforms 'raided' Moran's headquarters and executed seven members with machine guns and shotguns. Within days Capone received a summons to appear before a Grand Jury.

Al Capone

A series of trials followed. Capone's defence team bungled his defence but it was reflective of Capone's state of mind. At 32 years of age he was already displaying the addled sense of reality that came with tertiary syphilis and cocaine addiction. Capone's fears of Chicago ironically forced him into extended jaunts to other cities, hiding with his closest associates, in rented apartments or hiring complete Pullman cars on trains for security. It wasn't the gangs that caught him, it was the law. His first imprisonment was in Philadelphia for carrying a gun. Charges of vagrancy followed in Miami (Capone had no registered bank account) but the critical moment came when charges of tax evasion were upheld and Capone was sentenced to a record breaking 11 years.

In prison in Atlanta, then moving to Alcatraz and the Terminal Island, California, Capone lasted eight years before being released on medical grounds. Returning to Palm Island, Florida he died at home, as was his wish, in his bed, from cardiac arrest. He was 48.

Ironically, he contracted syphilis on his first trip to Chicago, in a brothel run by Johnny Torrio. He lies at Mount Carmel with the likes of Sam Giancana, Frank Nitti and Earl Hymie Weiss, the leader of the North Side gang.

LEE HARVEY OSWALD
(1939–1963)

SHANNON ROSE HILL
MEMORIAL PARK, FORT WORTH,
TEXAS, USA

The grave of Lee Harvey Oswald, assassin of US President John F. Kennedy, is marked with a simple rose granite headstone embedded in the lawn of Rose Hill Cemetery. The original stone stolen, it is fortunate that any marker exists for such an infamous individual. No mourners attended his funeral in 1963 and the press gallery were 'press-ganged' into acting as pall bearers as he was laid to rest on the same day the nation buried Kennedy. Such was the hatred directed towards the man that fired on President Kennedy from the Texas Book Depository on November 22, 1963.

Described as a withdrawn and temperamental child he had been diagnosed as having, passive aggressive schizoid features that needed continued treatment. Oswald was born in New Orleans but the early death of his father destabilised the family's existence and by the age of 17 they had moved to 22 different locations and Oswald had attended 12 schools.

He joined the Marines at age 17 and although slight in stature he seemed to have

found a niche. He was rated as a sharpshooter initially and later as a marksman but his nascent personality problems surfaced and he was court-martialed three times. While in the Marines, his dissatisfaction with life began to resurface and he became fascinated with the possibility of a living in a 'perfect society' in Soviet Russia. He manipulated a hardship discharge from the Marines and travelled to the Soviet Union and asked to become a Soviet Citizen. His reception was viewed suspiciously and he wounded himself, forcing the Soviet authorities to keep him under psychiatric assessment. Once recovered, he presented himself to the US embassy in Moscow and renounced his US citizenship. The Soviets took up his offer and his defection made headlines in the US.

His infatuation with Russia, its women and lifestyle soured soon after and he wrote requesting a return of his passport, which had never formally been revoked. He returned to the US, with his new Russian bride in 1962.

Oswald came back to Dallas and Fort Worth. Here, he drifted between low-level jobs but his abiding interest was Marxist politics, particularly attached to the US Cuban policy. It is during this phase that Oswald crossed paths with characters from New Orleans who were surreptitiously attached to the espionage industry, notably Guy Bannister, David Ferrie and George DeMohrenschildt.

In March, 1963 Oswald acquired two weapons using the alias 'A. Hiddell' – a Mannlicher-Carcano rifle and a Smith and Wesson .38. These weapons featured in the assassination attempt on Edwin Walker in April 1963, the murder of police officer J.D Tippit and the assassination of J.F.K. In the month before the assassination Oswald had travelled to Mexico City to try and gain entry to Cuba but had been refused.

In the week before the assassination, Oswald had asked a co-worker for a mid-week lift to his home to Irving to pick up 'curtain rods'. The plan had been hatched; Oswald had the Carcano stashed in his room. The President's motorcade was to pass the book depository where he had picked up a lowly paid job, the route clearly shown in Dallas newspapers. The opportunity had come for Oswald to live the larger life, to be a man of note in the world and to shape the world that he had failed to understand. Now the world would turn, as he wanted it.

Three shots were fired from the Texas Book Depository. Oswald made his escape after establishing an alibi by going to the lunchroom. He made his way to his boarding house, picked up the .38 and was making his way on foot when Police Officer J.D. Tippit stopped him. He shot Tippit four times and escaped into the Texas Theatre where he was arrested.

Two days later, on November 24, 1963 after questioning by Dallas police and FBI, Oswald was being led to the County jail when the second most famous assassination was shown on live television. Dallas nightclub owner Jack Ruby fired a single shot at close range. Oswald died in the same hospital, Parkland Memorial, as JFK had two days previously, silenced by Ruby.

Conspiracy theories still abound and deservedly so. Some of the Warren Commission files remained sealed but this much we know … Ruby had made three attempts to get to Oswald before that fateful day and he was heavily connected to organised crime figures. In the 1970s, the Unites States House Select Committee on Assassinations found in favour with what most people believed, that JFK was most likely killed by a conspiracy. Today, with a wealth of forensic information published, one cannot be so sure.

Lee Harvey Oswald

JACK RUBY
(1911–1967)

WESTLAWN CEMETERY,
ILLINOIS, USA

A nondescript rose granite headstone and a simple epitaph belie the notoriety of the man whose remains lie below. Jacob Leon Rubenstein aka Jack Ruby, died on January 3, 1967, awaiting a retrial for the murder of Lee Harvey Oswald. The murder committed in the Dallas police headquarters as Oswald was being transferred to the county jail was shown on live television on the NBC network. A small man about to make US history, Ruby was waiting for Oswald and launched himself onto the world stage with one rash action. In doing so, he forever clouded the most famous assassination in the 20th century, and the possible connections to elements of the US community that may well have conspired to kill the President.

Ruby's story is familiar; he came from a large family, was uncontrollable from a young age and often truant from school, he spent time in foster homes. Falling quickly into the petty street crime that characterised Chicago's streets (usually illegal gambling), Ruby soon became attached to the International Brotherhood of Teamsters. The war intervened and he served honourably, but after his discharge

he fell back into his familiar pattern and moved to Dallas in 1947 to manage strip clubs, dance halls and nightclubs.

Despite arrests for petty violations of licensing and liquor laws he had close ties to Dallas Police Department officers and organised crime figures. He travelled to Cuba in 1959 and was reported to have been gunrunning on the behalf of Mafia boss Santo Trafficante. The House Select Committee on Assassinations deemed in 1976 that Ruby was most likely 'a courier' for gambling interests, despite the Warren Commission dismissing his connections to organised crime. It is these kind of contradictions that fuel Ruby's notoriety.

Seth Kantor, a White House correspondent, claims that he saw Ruby in Parkland Hospital just after the assassination of JFK and was often seen in the halls of Dallas police headquarters after the arrest of Oswald. At 11:21am on November 24, as Oswald was being escorted to an armoured car, Ruby stepped from the crowd and shot him in the abdomen yelling, rather lamely, 'You killed the President, you rat!'. Ruby was wrestled to the ground.

The act was disturbing, shaking an already traumatised nation. Murder on live television would never have been contemplated in the sixties and Ruby's actions, characterised as a patriot wanting to spare Jacki Kennedy the ignominy of a public trial, served only to complicate the matter. Very few have ever believed that Ruby acted out of a sense of nobility and outrage, (his legal team claimed he wanted to 'redeem the city of Dallas' in the eyes of the world), but other elements of Ruby's life fuelled suspicion.

Incredibly, entry into the basement of the Dallas police headquarters was far too easy on the morning of Oswald's transfer and security was actually removed before the shooting. There is also evidence that the Dallas police department withheld evidence from the Warren Commission, perhaps from a sense of embarrassment. Lastly, evidence of Ruby's connections to organised crime (Sam Giancana, Carlos Marcello, Jimmy Hoffa, Joseph Campisi, Tony Accardo). These men despised JFK for his policies in Cuba and his brother Bobby's crackdown on criminal activity in the US, all this was more than enough for some to draw the conclusion that Oswald's death, like that of Kennedy, was a 'mob hit'.

Ruby continually asked to speak to the Warren Commission and to be taken

Jack Ruby

to Washington DC for protection. The Warren Commission denied his requests. He maintained after his conviction that 'everything pertaining to what's happened has never come to the surface...' and claimed that Kennedy's assassination was a coup and that he was used 'for a pourpose' (sic). If he knew more, as he intimated, he never got the chance to tell his story.

Riddled with cancer, Jack Ruby died of a pulmonary embolism at Parkland Hospital in 1967 where Kennedy and Oswald also died. He is buried with his parents in the Westlawn Cemetery, in Norridge, Illinois ... a petty criminal who would have disappeared nameless and unknown other than for his spurious actions in the Dallas police headquarters on November 24, 1963.

Jack Ruby

Chapter Eight

ANTIQUITY

CAESAR AUGUSTUS
(63BC—AD14)

MAUSOLEUM OF AUGUSTUS, PIAZZA AUGUSTO IMPERATORE, ROME, ITALY

The vast circular building near the Via di Ripetta, 42 metres in height, 90 metres in diameter, its roof held by twin pink granite obelisks housed the remains of the man that shaped the Rome we know and see. Having found Rome made of clay, he left it made of marble. The first true emperor of Rome, Gauis Octavius was born on the September 23, 63 BC. His father had died when he was four but his mother's connection was to be of much greater importance, she was sister to Julius Caesar.

Octavian was short of stature and of poor health but charismatic, loyal and determined. He served with Caesar in Spain in 46 BC and took control of a Parthian expedition in 44 BC when he heard of Caesar's assassination. He returned and demanded retribution for Caesar despite Antony's call for amnesty. His stand was popular amongst Caesar's legions and the Roman mob. Although young Octavian seized the opportunity to make war on Antony and defeated him at Mutina, the civil war that followed claimed the conspirators and Cicero and left Octavian,

Antony and Lepidus in an uneasy peace; the Roman world divided amongst them. Octavian in charge of the West, Antony the East and Lepidus Africa.

The truce did not last long and Antony's lavish kingly behaviour in Egypt, with his consort Cleopatra, inflamed the strict moral duty of the Romans and when Antony's will declared his allegiances with Cleopatra, the Senate declared war. Antony was destroyed at the sea battle at Actium. Octavian was emperor in all but name. He was 36.

Octavian was more than aware of Caesar's fate and moved to return all his powers and titles to the Senate, who promptly reinstated them. The Romans were tired of 15 years of civil war and bestowed on Octavian enough power to consolidate his position for a decade and eventually for life. To maintain the love of the people he rebuilt the city, amused the mob, built aqueducts and, sensibly, sent the legions from Italy to conquer territory, enlarging and enriching the Romans

Caesar Augustus

and keeping Rome safe from ambitious generals.

Octavian's other great asset was his general Lepidus who managed Octavian's battles and his friend Agrippa whose loyalty was unquestioned. He knew that he must be decisive and so took high moral ground on many issues, exiling unruly relatives and ensuring the succession. His longevity produced for the Romans, stability and for Augustus as he was now known, the further title of 'pater patriae' – father of the country. During his final years he withdrew more and more from public life and allowed his adopted son Tiberius the responsibilities of governing. He fell ill on a journey to Capri and died on August 19, 14 AD. He was 76.

His heirs and descendants, the Julio-Claudian emperors would go on to become the most notorious of the ancient world – forgetting the legacy of Augustus.

His ashes were sealed in a cinerary urn and placed in the massive mausoleum that be began building in 28 BC. The ashes were stolen and debased, according to legend, by the Visigoths.

PHARAOH KHUFU
(?–2566BC)

THE GREAT PYRAMID OF GIZA, EGYPT

'I am protected of Horus/ He protects me. He who crushes the enemies of Horus'. The claim characterises the man. At once a servant and an equal of a god, the builder of the greatest tomb in the world, Pharaoh Khufu, built The Great Pyramid of Giza 61 centuries ago, it stands on the Giza plateau near Cairo. A building whose immensity guarantees its existence beyond human civilization, the method of its creation is uncertain but even in Roman times it was considered 'the idle and foolish ostentation of royal wealth'. Records agree that at least 100,000 workers were used in 'shifts' of three-month intervals over a 20-year period to complete the pyramid. We can only guess at the methods and wielding of such power that reset a nation's economy to achieve such an end.

Khufu died in 2566BC. The length of his reign is disputed, but generally considered to be at least 23 years, of which 20 were dedicated to the construction of the pyramid and associated structures. Details of Khufu's reign are scant outside the necropolis of Giza but shipping records point to a Pharaoh driven to

acquire and accumulate turquoise, cedar and copper – the most expensive and highly sought after commodities of the world of antiquity – all featuring in the elaborate funerary preparations for the afterlife of the Egyptian elite.

The pyramid and necropolis was set at the northern end of the Giza plateau. The extent and size of the pyramid too great to be supported by the loosened stones further south and was named 'the horizon of Khufu'. It was surrounded by an elaborate network of funerary chapels and mortuary chapels, built of fine black basalt, red granite and with ceilings of polished limestone.

The dimensions of the Great Pyramid are staggering, 230 metres square and 140 metres tall, but it had been higher, capped with a highly polished pyramidion, lost through stone theft, that had the pyramid shimmer in bright white light. It was constructed from roughly hewn blocks of dark limestone and this is the core that is visible today. The inner walls and chambers are of polished granite.

The structure of the internals of the pyramid are fascinating. Three chambers – at the top, the king's burial chamber, in the middle, the statue chamber (often erroneously called the queen's chamber), and below ground and unfinished, the underworld chamber. The king's burial chamber features a massive granite sarcophagus. The great gallery, leading to the king's chamber is almost nine metres high and 50 metres long and has an important architectural function of redistributing weight into the core.

What kind of man diverts the wealth of a nation to build a machine designed to defeat death? In essence, little is known of Khufu. Ancient sources depict him as cruel and rapacious. His control of society and the generation of immense wealth during the reigns of the pharaohs of the Fourth dynasty point to a bent by Khufu's predecessors and his successors to institute a life dedicated to becoming divine, to sit with the gods equally in the Afterlife. We still marvel and are awestruck at the capabilities of humans in such distant past.

The irony is that the ultimate glory of the horizon of Khufu is that we don't see it in its glory. The common people of Cairo have for centuries and centuries plundered the pyramid, their humble limestone dwellings built from the stone stripped from the house of a god.

TUTANKHAMUN
(1342—1323BC)

THE VALLEY OF THE KINGS,
EGYPT

In many respects the most extraordinary tomb of all is not the sculpted magnificence of Europe or imposing monuments of America, but a hastily crafted secret chamber, hewn from rock. At the end of a passageway, filled with discarded rock chips and stone refuse – the tomb of the Boy King, Tutankhamun. The only extant tomb of a pharaoh ever found, filled with 'Wonderful things,' as famously remarked by its discoverer, Howard Carter.

Slight of build, but tall for the times (180 centimetres) the young pharaoh had disappeared from history until the discovery of his tomb. The last in line of the famous Thutmosid pharaohs, records of his existence had been hacked away from the monuments of 14th century BC Egypt. His father had been a religious heretic and his advisors had started a damaging civil war after his death. His short reign became legend and myth.

Tutankhamun became pharaoh at age nine and was dead by 19. His wife and

sister had produced two stillborn children and so his line ended with his death. He rejected his father's religious heresy and abandoned the astonishing capital his father had created for the worship of Aten the sun god, changing his name to reflect his faith and restoring the faith of people, priest and advisors. Despite his age, he is said to have engaged in external wars and to have had a violent temper but his great interest for those of the modern world was to provide an insight into the ancient world of Egypt.

The discovery of the tomb gripped the world's imagination. Howard Carter's discovery in 1922 was the culmination of eight years work, and a last ditch attempt creating 'Egyptomania', particularly in England and America. Within the tomb, the world of Tutankhamun had been recreated, the most magnificent of funerary accoutrements to accompany him into the afterlife and establish his place amongst the gods. A golden sarcophagus, a funerary mask of unsurpassed beauty, the embalmed bodies of his children and an immense quantity of the possessions of the young king: campaign seats, a chariot, hunting bows, walking sticks. A travelling exhibition of the material, now largely housed in the Cairo Museum, has been a regular event but the king still lies in the tomb, rarely exhibited

The condition of the tomb suggested an unexpected death and a rushed burial – the key to its survival intact. DNA analysis has revealed much of the medical history of the king and it is thought that he died from an infected broken leg, exacerbated by his malaria and certain congenital flaws, deriving from incest. It seems his body was burnt, spontaneously combusting through chemical reaction – more evidence of a hasty burial, as there is visible splotching on some of the art work – indicating it was wet at the time the tomb was sealed.

The discovery spawned an industry in popular culture that is unabated. But the curse of the 'Mummy' is, statistically, a fraud. There is no difference between the fate of those that entered the tomb and those that did not. Howard Carter died in 1939 at age 64, his granite funerary monument at Putney Vale Cemetery, elegantly graced with the lines, 'O night, spread they wings over me as the imperishable stars'. A quote from the Wishing Cup of Tutankhamun, truly one of the most 'wonderful things' in the world, the gift of his discovery, a moment in the world of an ancient king.

QIN SHI HUANG
(259–210BC)

MAUSOLEUM OF THE FIRST QIN EMPEROR, SHAANXI, CHINA

Guarding their emperor, Qin Shi Huang, is a silent army of 8000 warriors, of all ranks and varied appearance, holding weaponry that defied 2000 years. Their swords remain sharpened and ready for the long battle and a sober warning for those who sought to defile his tomb.

The figures of the 'Terracotta Army' were discovered in 1974 by farmers who were digging water wells 1.6 kilometres to the east of the Qin Emperor's burial mound at Mount Li (Lashan). In addition, an entire necropolis was found surrounding the burial mound. The mound itself was a pyramidal shape, constructed as a microcosm of his palace, in much the same pattern as other monumental architecture from the Mediterranean. The tomb of Zheng itself remains unopened, the excuse is concern for the preservation of its artefacts so the real testament to Zheng's greatness are the extant 'warriors'. These were constructed in a primitive but effective assembly line process, where face moulds and other 'body' parts were constructed and then assembled to give the appearance in individuation.

Terracotta fragments had been found for centuries near the site and had been considered worthless and simply discarded. Underground watercourses and jade were abundant in the area and the terracotta was considered a nuisance. These fragments are believed to have derived from the sacking of one part of the necropolis (in Pit 1 and 2) and the burning of the timber roof that housed the army, the timbers falling and shattering the pieces. Some weaponry is missing from these areas of the excavation site.

China's first emperor was Qin Shi Huang (personal name Zheng). He united the warring states of China by conquest. He subdued the states to the east and south, barricaded the new Empire behind the Great Wall and protected his empire from attack from the north and north-west. He built the Lingqa canal to link north and south and supply his armies. He famously spent many years searching for the 'Elixir of Immortality'. His obsession may explain the elaborate detail and immensity of his mausoleum and funerary preparations.

Zheng died during one of his tours of eastern China on September 10, 210BC at the Shaqiu palace after ingesting mercury pills, prescribed by one of his alchemists. He was fascinated by the properties of mercury, his tomb is said to have contained a replica of the 100 rivers of China, expressed in mercury and the surrounds of his burial tomb contain high levels of the metal. His Prime Minister Li Si was so concerned that the Emperor's death would cause a general uprising that his death was concealed. The journey back to Xianyang took two months during which time the Emperors clothes were changed daily, his face shaded from all onlookers and two barrels of rotting fish were carried before and after the Emperor's wagon to disguise the smell of decomposition.

Zheng's elixir for immortality was not to be found in the concoction of some necromancer, but at the foot of Mount Li, guarded by his silent army, fixed for all time and guaranteeing we remember and revere him.

HADRIAN
(76–138AD)

HADRIAN'S TOMB, CASTEL SANT'ANGELO, PARCO ADRIANO, ROME, ITALY

The great architect and builder of the Roman Empire, in the literal sense, Hadrian stabilised the empire and established its extent. He is best known for his set of fortifications in Britain, as well as his mausoleum – a cylindrical building known now as the Castel Sant'Angelo, erected on the right bank of the Tiber between 134 and 139 AD. The mausoleum originally held the remains of Hadrian and his family and succeeding emperors until the death of Caracalla. The urns and ashes contained in the mausoleum were scattered by the Visigoths during Alaric's sacking the city in 410 AD.

The funerary urn of Hadrian, and the stone columns of his tomb were incorporated into St Peter's basilica, symbolising the successful sublimation of the ancient pagan world into the Christian world.

The 'Castel Sant'Angelo' takes its name from the alledged appearance of the archangel Michael, atop of the mausoleum. It was reported that he was seen

sheathing his sword of vengeance, a signal that the plague that destroyed much of the Roman population had ended and a vindication of Pope Gregory's destruction of ancient pagan sites of worship.

Hadrian is considered one of the 'Five Good Emperors'. He came to the throne in dubious circumstances, being adopted and chosen as emperor by Plotina, the wife of the emperor Trajan who 'favoured' Hadrian. It was she who signed the adoption and succession.

Hadrian spent little of his reign in Rome. He was a philhellene, adoring Greek cultural achievements and style, adopting Athens as his favoured city. Much of the architecture below the Acropolis was commissioned and designed by Hadrian. He was also a supreme negotiator and his reign was distinguished by a restoration of peace (*Pax Romana*) with the exception of the second Jewish War. The brutality was such that he was cursed in Aramaic with the epitaph 'may his bones be crushed'.

It was his controversial love for the Bithynian youth, Antinous, that outraged Roman society. He is said to have wept like 'a woman' when Antinous drowned in the Nile, allegedly as part of a ritualised religious offering. Hadrian had Antinous deified, a process only accorded to Roman emperors and their families. Antinous travelled with Hadrian and his wife Sabina, and their entourage, including architects, builders, poets as well as the formidable military contingent. It was after Antinous' death that Hadrian undertook his campaign against the Jews. Hadrian was grief stricken and his health declined from this point.

His final years conform to what we expect from Roman Emperors, intrigue and a loss of popularity, attempted coups and deaths of opponents. Hadrian's health had deteriorated to such an extent that he often asked slaves to put him to the sword, only to be saved by his family. He died of heart failure on July 10, 138 AD. He was first buried at Puteoli, near Baiae and his remains were then transferred to the Gardens of Domitia, close to the mausoleum, to await its completion. His remains were then cremated and his ashes placed with those of his wife Sabina and his first adoptive son Lucius. He was deified in 139 AD and given a temple on the Campus Martius.

He embodied what we remember of the Romans now; their grandeur, power,

idiosyncrasies and what they became. His mausoleum was the tallest building in Rome, symbolising his influence over the Romans and their reverence for him.

Hadrian

SELDEC OSSUARY
(1200s)

SEDLEC OSSUARY (THE BONE CATHEDRAL), SEDLEC, CZECH REPUBLIC

Rather than being the tomb of a notable historical figure or the memorial to a horrific event or moment in time, the Sedlec Ossuary is an extraordinary reminder of the hold over the medieval mind of religion and an odd perception of religious faith. Its innate appeal demonstrates a fascination with death that struck through all levels of medieval society and its appeal today ranges from curiosity to horror. It attracts over 200,000 visitors per year.

The Sedlec Ossuary (Kostnice v Sedlec) is a small Roman Catholic chapel, originally a simple funerary chapel located beneath the Cemetery Church of All Saints in a suburb of Kutna Hora in the Czech Republic, 77 kilometres to the east of Prague. The ossuary is believed to contain the remains of between 40,000 and 70,000 people. It is the appearance and arrangement of these remains that distinguish the chapel from any other in Christendom. Visitors move down a short flight of limestone steps and are presented with a unique arrangement of

the remains of the blessed. Four enormous bell shaped mounds made of skulls, occupy the four corners of the chapel.

The walls and arches are adorned with human bones arranged in a bizarre set of still lives that annotate the role of death in Christian existence. An enormous chandelier, containing at least one of every human bone hangs from the nave. The garlands that usually accompany such displays, celebrating life and symbolising the Christian journey to redemption here replaced with skulls, draping the vault with an off putting reminder of mortality. The display continues with the altar flanked with monstrances and the Schwarzenberg coat of arms contrived with skeletons. The last designer of the display, Frantisek Rint, a woodcarver, has his name executed in bone at the entrance to the chapel.

In 1278, Henry, Abbot of the Cistercian monastery in Sedlec was sent by his King Ottokar II, the Iron and Golden king of Bohemia, to the Holy Land on a mission to bring a blessing from the Holy Land. The king was a stalwart of the Crusades and the mission a defiance of the threat from the Muslim East. Henry returned with earth collected from the hill of Golgotha, the place of Christ's crucifixion that was duly sprinkled on the abbey cemetery. The word spread quickly throughout Central Europe and the Abbey Cemetery became a desired burial site.

The onset of the Black Death in the 14th century saw the enlargement of the cemetery to accommodate the desires of those dying and those that fell in the Hussite wars of the following century. A Gothic church was built in the cemetery and the lower level became the ossuary, storing the remains for reburial or moved to find space for Europe's elite that sought burial in such holy ground. The numbers were staggering and eventually, Rint was charged by the Schwarzenberg family with ordering the bones to create some meaning for those that came and those housed here. The result is the truly extraordinary and although we cannot name those who lay here, where they lay the world of death was never more curiously and frighteningly presented.

The ossuary is widely referenced in Czech literature and the gothic realm of world literature. It is an experience not to be underestimated in impact on individuals and cultures alike.

SAINT JOHN OF NEPOMUK
(1340–1393)

St Vitus Cathedral, Prague, Czech Republic

John of Nepomuk or John Nepomucen is the patron saint of the Czechs although statues of the saint are widely distributed in Central Europe. He represents the struggle of the oppressed against oppressors and his torture and murder by King Wenceslaus is symbolic of the battle of individuals to overcome corrupted values of the powerful against the meek. He is also revered as a saint for the extraordinary occurrence of the opening of his tomb 300 years after his death that revealed the living tongue of John, vibrant and uncorrupted. The uproar of the announcement reverberated in Europe and not debunked until 1973 when the tongue was found to be a part of St John's brain, itself an extraordinary moment. His tomb itself is the largest single sculpture of silver and silver gilt in the world, weighing one and a half tonnes.

John was born at Nepomuk in Bohemia in 1340 and died in March 1393. Contemporaneous documents contend that John was Vicar-General of the archdiocese of Prague and had flagrantly disobeyed the wishes of King

Wenceslaus IV. John had appointed a successor to the Abbot of Prague without consultation to the king, correct procedure in canonical law but his actions had enraged Wenceslaus IV. The king had promised the position, and the progression of the Abbey into a cathedral to one of his favourites. Wenceslaus, as Holy Roman Emperor, was a very powerful figure but his power was constantly challenged by the Bohemian nobility and particularly within his own family. His manipulation of the investiture of the abbot and the cruel torture and murder of John precipitated a rebellion.

John and other members of the Abbey hierarchy were burnt as torture but would not demur and John was marched through the city in secrecy, his tongue silenced with a block of wood, he was sown into a goatskin and thrown from the Charles Bridge into the Vlatva to drown.

The countryside was plunged into a drought, seen as retribution from God, and a year later John's body was found and Wenceslaus's treachery discovered.

Saint John of Nepomuk

Wenceslaus was deposed. John's body was interred in the Abbey. Official documents begun to refer to John as 'martyr Sanctus' less than 50 years after his death. Historians of the 16th and 17th centuries maintain that John was also punished for not violating the sanctity of the confessional. John as confessor to Wenceslaus' wife would not cooperate with the monarch who he suspected of an affair. The cathedral that replaced the abbey was completed in 1727 and stands as the greatest example of the unique Bohemian Baroque.

Whatever the truth of John's existence and death, his tomb stands as testament to the uniqueness of morality, cast against power politics. St Vitus' cathedral houses a most unique tomb, amongst the staggering beauty of this place.

His tomb sits amongst many Bohemian kings and Holy Roman Emperors, amongst the sacred and profane.

TAJ MAHAL
(1632–1653)

TAJ MAHAL, AGRA UTTAR PRADESH, INDIA

Rather than being dedicated to the search for immortality or the vainglorious, the Taj Mahal is dedicated to love. Built over a period of 21 years, the Mausoleum and its attendant structures were inspired by the Shah Jahan's love for his wife, Mumtaz Mahal, a Persian princess who died whilst giving birth to her 14th child. The Shah was distraught at her death and wrote of the Taj and his wife, 'The sight of this mansion creates sorrowing sighs, and the sun and the moon shed tears from their eyes'.

The tomb is, understandably, the focal point for the Taj Mahal. A large white marble structure it is a symmetrical building of octagonal shape, featuring an arched doorway, a dome of 35 metres in height, surrounded by smaller mimicking kiosks, emphasising its shape. The main chamber features the false sarcophagi of the Shah Jahan and Mumtaz Mahal, the actual graves are below ground. The compound is surrounded by minarets each 40 metres tall. The external decorations are astounding, designs in the Islamic and Persian tradition in tracery

and inlay of precious and semi-precious stones.

This astonishing building was created by the richest Mughal emperor of India, his reign known as the Golden age. The prosperity of his reign reflected in the opulence of design and execution. The Taj is built on a reclaimed parcel of land, levelled at 50 metres above the river. A fifteen-kilometre ramp was built to bring marble and materials, marble from Rajasthan, jade and crystal from China, turquoise from Tibet. Teams of oxen between 20 and 30 hauled what was needed for 21 years as well as 1000 elephants, the total cost estimated to 32 million rupees at the time.

The Shah gained the throne after his military successes as a prince. Mughal succession was not guaranteed and contenders had to prove themselves. He turned his successes in the south against rebel forces quickly to his advantage and received the throne from his father in 1628. He promptly executed his rivals and imprisoned his stepmother. He was a vigorous defender of the Faith and lacked the moderate policies towards non-Muslims that his predecessors had adopted and led wars against the Sultanates, the Ottomans and the Portuguese. It was with his brothers that the end of his reign would come.

He became ill and placed his son as regent. This infuriated his brothers, particularly Aurangzeb who met him in battle, defeated him and placed him under house arrest for eight years until his death. This was shortly after the completion of the Taj. His view from the Agra fort was across the river to the 'crown of palaces', the resting place of his beloved.

POPE INNOCENT X1
(1611–1689)

St Peter's Basilica, Rome, Italy

Uncorrupted and incorruptible, an example for the modern Church but living three centuries ago, Benedetto Odescalchi became Innocent XI and cowered the most powerful monarchs in Europe. He withstood the Ottoman invasion but perhaps is best remembered for his exhumation where, after 267 years his body was preserved and intact and the miracle exposed his remains to the world in the most beautiful church in the world.

Born into nobility in Como on May 16, 1611, Benedetto was educated by Jesuits. His mother was killed by plague in 1630, his father died four years earlier so he joined with his uncles in banking who had developed a very lucrative business in European cities. Benedetto became disillusioned with his career and between 1632 and 1636 moved to Rome and sought to serve the Church. His intelligence and connections saw him rise to the rank of Cardinal. He was sent to Ferarra and became known as the 'father of the poor'. By 1650 he was Bishop of Novara and a strong papal candidate on the death of Clement IX but was opposed by the Louis

XIV of France. After the death of Clement X, the French influence acquiesced and he was made Pope in 1676.

He immediately began reforming the Church, curtailing excessive spending (his experience in finance was invaluable) and shifted the emphasis of the papacy from opulence to frugality and the poor. The Church's finances improved dramatically and its influence in politics increased. He brought German states closer to Papal influence to counter the strength of France and used the new strength of the Church to fund wars against the invading Ottomans, particularly in the Battle of Vienna where the city had been besieged. He challenged French power by disclaiming the right of asylum for foreign ambassadors in Rome, a privilege that had been open to abuse. He made substantial attacks on the morality issues in Rome; at the time rife with prostitution and gambling – even changing dress codes for women – and insisted on education programs for all. He was a thoroughly 'modern' influence and this element, in part, led to his beatification.

Innocent XI died on August 12, 1689 after a long deterioration in health of kidney failure. He was buried in St Peter's Basilica beneath his funeral monument near the Clementine Chapel, the monument characterises his support for Vienna. The process of beatification began in 1691 but was suspended, through French influence, until 1956! When exhumed his body was found to be incorrupt and his body was placed in a glass sarcophagus under the Altar of St Sebastian and then to the Altar of Transfiguration.

He has become a beacon of faith whom abhorred the corruption of the Church and his body, incorrupt, stands as symbol to the power of purity of intention and is a sight to see.

MEDICI CHAPELS
(1600s-1700s)

BASILICA OF SAN LORENZO,
FLORENCE, ITALY

The most powerful family in Europe for three centuries, whose blood runs in the veins of kings and popes, Grand Dukes of Tuscany, demanded the most magnificent of funerary crypts. Who to design and carve their resting place for eternity than the most magnificent of sculptors, Michelangelo. The Medici Chapels in Florence at the Basilica of San Lorenzo are the Sagrestia Nuova and the Cappella Dei Principi.

The Medicis had established a sophisticated control of clothing manufacturing through various guilds, based on a franchise system that saw them directly, and often more importantly, indirectly responsible for the employment of at least half of the population of Florence. This system was augmented by the development of a powerful banking structure, using the double entry system of tracking debits and credits (discovered by mathematician, Luca Pacioli, Da Vinci's intimate). Their influence in Europe was unsurpassed and although many of the family held no official position, their control over the Papacy (the family produced four popes)

and politics was undeniable and corrupt. Even when the leaders of the family were exiled, second tier family members maintained their influence until the return of the family. In this way and with popular support from the rising merchant class ensured their dominance of the 14th and 15th century in particular, the High Renaissance.

The most renowned of the Medicis was Lorenzo the Magnificent, the subject of a complex assassination plot in 1478 that resulted in the death of his brother. The plot included other prominent families but significantly, the Archbishop of Pisa and the Pope, who gave the plotters dispensation for crimes done in the service of the Church. Periods of exile and civil unrest did not stop the Medicis from controlling Italian politics; position in the Papacy ensured their power through the 16th century via Leo X and Clement VII and eventually to having cousins marry into the royal families of France and Spain.

Michelangelo had completed the sculptures for the Sagrestia, thematically named and position as times of day (Night and Day, Dusk and Dawn) but the chapel wasn't completed until 1555 by order of Cosimo I. The result is that this magnificent tomb is that of the unimportant Duke of Urbino, and the Duke of Nemours. With that Lorenzo lies beneath the altar at the entrance but on an unfinished wall in Michelangelo's masterpiece, 'Madonna and Child' overseeing all the Medicis. His design drawings were found in a concealed corridor in 1976.

The Cappella dei Principi is dominated by a 59-metre dome and formulated by Cosimo I and was a collaborative design, true court art. The marble walls are inlaid with semi-precious stones, covering the entire surface but within the chapel the six sarcophagi are empty, the remains of the Medicis interred below in the crypt. Those that had built the enormous wealth of Florence and funded the great artists of the Renaissance are, ironically, unable to see their magnificence.

AUSCHWITZ-BIRKENAU (1940–1945)

AUSCHWITZ-BIRKENAU, CONCENTRATION CAMP, POLAND

No more sobering experience in the world than to stand at the gates of Auschwitz and read its bitter irony of 'Arbeit mach frei' and to understand that 1.5 million souls naïvely passed beneath. Established in 1979 as a UNESCO World heritage site recognising the worst excess of human depravity. Not a tomb of magnificence, the site has been maintained as a shell that depicts, in the imagination, moments of horror to remind the world 'never again.'

Auschwitz was a complex of 45 different camps, serving the interests of the Reich and enacting the madness of Nazi racial policy. Originally a Polish army barracks, the Nazis had annexed Poland and began to search for a facility to house political prisoners. The SS, who administered the camp, isolated a 40 square kilometre space, surrounding the barracks with electrified fence and confiscated all on site buildings. Success on the battlefield delivered Soviet prisoners – 10,000 arrived in 1941 – by May only 900 survived, disease and starvation took their toll.

By 1942 the 'Final Solution' had been determined and Auschwitz-Birkenau was designated as the primary site to accomplish the task.

Auschwitz served as a trial. The first gas chamber – the red house – was a gutted cottage. It demonstrated the logistics of dealing with mass death, the disposal of bodies, the recycling of possessions (including dental work, glasses and hair). The methodology established, Birkenau was purpose built with four crematoria and a single railway spur (the Way of Death) to deliver over 900,000 in 1944 when Hungarian Jews arrived en masse.

Not only remembered for the horror of numbers, Auschwitz is remembered for the unspeakable manner of death – medical experiments, deliberate use of typhus and noma to control numbers and the horror of the gas chamber itself – the screams of realisation as the pellets dropped, the degradation.

The looming presence of the Red Army in late 1944 saw the destruction of the camp by the SS guards under direction from Himmler who wanted all evidence – administrative and human – destroyed. His order was that no one should be able to determine how many had died. 58,000 were marched to Bergen-Belsen, 20,000 survived and were liberated.

When Soviet forces arrived in Auschwitz they found 7,500 prisoners and 600 corpses, 375,000 men's suits, 837,000 women's garments and 7.7 tonnes of human hair (to be used for carpeting). Soviet investigators uncovered the horrors over the next 12 years. The Commander of the camp, Rudolf Höss, revealed much of the extermination process in his trial.

The gallows on which he was hanged stand close to the red house and within sight of the cottage where he lived with his wife and children, served by Jehovah's Witness detainees, preferred as house slaves for their non-violent attitude.

Amongst the Jews were political prisoners, homosexuals, and Romany (gypsies) whose word for their time in Auschwitz is 'porajimos' – the devouring.

First published in 2015 by New Holland Publishers Pty Ltd

London • Sydney • Auckland

The Chandlery Unit 009 50 Westminster Bridge Road London SE1 7QY United Kingdom
1/66 Gibbes Street Chatswood NSW 2067 Australia
5/39 Woodside Ave Northcote, Auckland 0627 New Zealand

www.newhollandpublishers.com
Copyright © 2015 New Holland Publishers Pty Ltd
Copyright © 2015 in text: Steve Cooper
Copyright © 2015 in images: Wiki Commons except pages 4-5 (Mary Evans Picture Libary)

A record of this book is held at the British Library and the National Library of Australia.
ISBN 9781742577364

Managing Director: Fiona Schultz
Publisher: Alan Whiticker
Project Editor: Holly Willsher
Designer: Andrew Quinlan
Production Director: Olga Dementiev
Printer: Toppan Leefung Printing Limited
10 9 8 7 6 5 4 3 2 1

Keep up with New Holland Publishers on Facebook
www.facebook.com/NewHollandPublishers

Acknowledgements
Many thanks to Alan Whiticker at New Holland Publishers and his team for their cooperation, encouragement and the opportunity to work on this and other projects. Thanks to my team, particularly Loni Cooper, for a hard and fast eye, and no compromise on quality. And genuine appreciation to those dedicated individuals around the planet, paid and unpaid, who inspire writers to reflect on the beauty and majesty of the monuments to the past and the people that inhabited them.